PITTSBURGH
Food Crawls

PITTSBURGH
Food Crawls

Shannon Daly

TOURING *the* **NEIGHBORHOODS**
ONE BITE *& LIBATION AT a* **TIME**

Globe
Pequot
GUILFORD, CONNECTICUT

Globe Pequot

An imprint of The Rowman & Littlefield Publishing Group, Inc.
4501 Forbes Blvd., Ste. 200
Lanham, MD 20706
www.rowman.com

Distributed by NATIONAL BOOK NETWORK

British Library Cataloguing in Publication Information available

Library of Congress Cataloging-in-Publication Data available

ISBN 978-1-4930-4570-9 (paper : alk. paper)
ISBN 978-1-4930-4571-6 (electronic)

♾™ The paper used in this publication meets the minimum requirements of American National Standard for Information Sciences—Permanence of Paper for Printed Library Materials, ANSI/NISO Z39.48-1992

This book is dedicated to my fabulous Grandma Jo,
the biggest bookworm I know.

Contents

Introduction

Pittsburgh is known for its hard-working locals, numerous sports championships, and, as of late, the food scene. Pittsburgh is home to three rivers, the Allegheny, Ohio, and Monongahela, which many refer to as "The Mon." These three rivers meet at what's called, "The Point," one of Pittsburgh's most iconic features. Point State Park is where the three rivers collide and where you can find the larger-than-life fountain that soars 200 feet into the sky. The fountain is a key component of our city's beautiful skyline, as it sits right in front of the beautiful skyscrapers that create our downtown neighborhood.

The 'Burgh is broken down into many different neighborhoods, each having its own unique presence and purpose in the city that bleeds black and gold. The locals here take care of one another and always welcome visitors with open arms. While Pittsburgh is considered to be a smaller city compared to other major cities, it is packed tight with bridges, hills, and neighborhoods—and, of course, the cuisine options are endless. Neighborhoods in and all around Pittsburgh are flooded with fine dining, casual eats, and "hole-in-the-wall" restaurants. Locals and tourists have a unique variety of choices when it comes to dining in the 'Burgh. Here is where putting french fries on everything is not only accepted but encouraged. Pizza toppings are sometimes served cold, and variations of the pierogi are often a staple. Not a potato fan? That's okay. Pittsburgh has come full circle, offering an extensive amount of cuisine options.

The love for potatoes isn't Pittsburgh's only quirk. We also have a love for chipped chopped ham and saving our parking spots with chairs. The saying "Kennywood is open" can make anyone blush, and being a Jagoff (i.e., someone with an unfavorable personality or annoying habits) is something no one wants to be. Pittsburgh has a beautiful skyline, an abundance of history, and so many places to explore. Finding the perfect spot to dine or grab a refreshing beverage is never an issue here. Pittsburgh is a welcoming city and will leave a loving impression on any visitor with its loyal locals. No matter your food preference, Pittsburgh has it and, luckily, it is most likely closer than you think. This book only scratches the surface of all the fantastic food finds the Steel City has to offer.

Follow the Icons

 If you eat something outrageous and don't take a photo for Instagram, did you really eat it? These restaurants feature dishes that are Instagram famous. These foods must be seen (and snapped) to be believed, and luckily they taste as good as they look!

 This icon means that sweet treats are ahead. Bring your sweet tooth to these spots for dessert first (or second or third).

 Cheers to a fabulous night out in Pittsburgh! These spots add a little glam to your grub and are perfect for marking a special occasion.

 Follow this icon when you're crawling for cocktails. This symbol points out the establishments that are best known for their great drinks. The food never fails here, but be sure to come thirsty, too!

 Pittsburgh is for brunch. Look for this icon when crawling with a crew that needs sweet and savory (or an excuse to drink before noon).

THE STRIP DISTRICT CRAWL

1. GAUCHO PARRILLA ARGENTINA, 1601 Penn Ave., Pittsburgh, (412) 709-6622, eat-gaucho.com

2. PRIMANTI BROS., 46 18th St., Pittsburgh, (412) 263-2142, primantibros.com

3. KAYA, 2000 Smallman St., Pittsburgh, (412) 261-6565, kaya.menu

4. SMALLMAN GALLEY, 54 21st St., Pittsburgh, (412) 517-6100, smallmangalley.org

5. PAMELA'S DINER, 60 21st St., Pittsburgh, (412) 281-6366, pamelasdiner.com

6. BAR MARCO, 2216 Penn Ave., Pittsburgh, (412) 471-1900, barmarcopgh.com

7. DIANOIA'S EATERY, 2549 Penn Ave., Pittsburgh, (412) 918-1875, dianoiaseatery.com

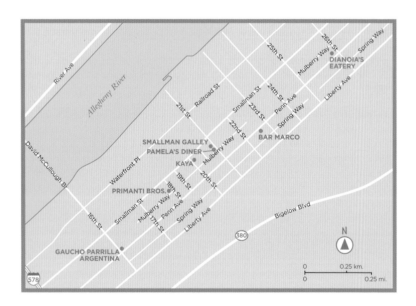

The Strip District

A Melting Pot of Cuisine

THE STRIP DISTRICT IS WHERE LOCALS COME TO EAT and shop and where visitors come to get a real taste of classic Pittsburgh. It's swarming with a mix of new and, shall I say, seasoned small businesses and family-owned storefronts. The Strip District is where anyone can indulge in specialty grocery stores, delis, and one-of-a-kind shops like the Pennsylvania Macaroni Company, Grandpa Joe's Candy Shop, or Roxanne's Dried Flowers. Pittsburgh pride attire can be found among fresh produce stands on nearly every street corner. Among these many gems are some of the city's best restaurants. Find a parking spot and take a long stroll down Penn Avenue and Smallman Street to truly enjoy this experience. You'll find the area to be especially jam-packed during weekend mornings, but this larger-than-life crowd is what makes the Strip District's world go round. With endless shopping, delicious coffee, warm baked goods, fresh produce, and vendors at every corner, the Strip District is a one-stop shop for all Pittsburgh favorites.

1 GAUCHO PARRILLA ARGENTINA

GAUCHO PARRILLA has been a Strip District fan favorite since the day it opened its doors back in early 2013. Designed as a counter-service restaurant, this place is one hot commodity in the Steel City. On a normal day for Gaucho, the line is out the door. This is a first-come, first-served facility, so during busy hours there will be a little wait. Gaucho is also BYOB, so grab a good bottle to pop and prepare to chill in line. Once you've made it inside and have placed your order, it's time to get excited. A staff member will help you find the perfect seat for your party, and the food will be brought out to you quickly.

Gaucho's Argentine-inspired menu is heavy on the flame-broiled meats, with options to spare. Sandwiches like the rosemary braised beef with caramelized onions and house-special horsey sauce, and the Vegetale with roasted beets, grilled eggplant, goat cheese, pickled onions, and arugula will satisfy any hungry palate. Too intimidated to pick up one of these jam-packed masterpieces? Gaucho isn't here to make anyone look bad—all sandwiches are available deconstructed with toast or sandwich bread. Just ask for "decon" instead of con pan. Small plates include the Picada ("seasonal pickins'") of meats, cheeses, and fruits), empanadas, and tostados. My personal favorite, the Provoletta, is worth the line even if it's down the block. The masters grill provolone cheese with fresh oregano on toast. Arugula and olive salad bring just the right Mediterranean bite to this cheesy goodness. Each and every option is loaded with flavor.

If you see the "End of the Line, Baby" sign out, be warned that you might not make it to the counter before closing. That said, make sure you're dining with people you can stand. It's worth it.

TIP

Skip the line by calling ahead for takeout!

2 PRIMANTI BROS.

Although this sandwich shop now has over 30 locations, back in 1933 PRIMANTI BROS. was just a little sandwich cart posted in the Strip. With the intention of selling to the hard-working truckers who were traveling in and out of the city, its sandwiches quickly became an iconic Pittsburgh staple, which today is craved by locals and intrigues visitors.

For those who need to catch up, Primanti's is known for its towering tall sandwiches that come loaded with french fries. Yes, you heard that right. If you're from Pittsburgh, or the least bit familiar with our cuisine, then you'll understand the normalcy of finding french fries piled on top of a sandwich or even a salad when ordering food in the 'Burgh.

Primanti Bros. can be found in many different places in and around the city, but the Strip District location is the original and the favorite. Aside from salads and popular bar appetizers like mozzarella wedges and spicy batter-dipped pickles, this menu is packed with sandwiches that satisfy

any hearty appetite. The lengthy list includes the Pitts-Burger & Cheese, Deluxe Double Egg & Cheese, Fried Jumbo Baloney & Cheese, and pastrami and cheese, just to name a few. Every sandwich is topped with french fries, coleslaw, and tomato. If you want onion, make sure to ask. It doesn't get more Pittsburgh than a sandwich at Primanti Bros.

3 KAYA

For over 20 years, KAYA has been channeling the tropics with flavors inspired by the Caribbean islands, South America, and beyond. The atmosphere in both the dining room and bar are exotic and welcoming. Even the sidewalk is lined with colorful tables that lend to the perfect outdoor dining experience. The food here is fun and comforting. The cocktails are another reason to head here ASAP. If you're not interested in a boozy cocktail but are still looking for something fresh, Kaya offers nonalcoholic refreshers that will do you just fine. These mocktails will treat your taste buds nicely but will still allow you to drive home safe!

The menu is loaded with Spanish classics while also incorporating some twists here and there. The

Kaya Fest is a block party with live music, dancing, and delicious street food. This is a ticketed event and totally worth every penny.

tropical paella will satisfy anyone's taste buds. Its ingredients include sofrito sauce, chicken, chorizo, scallops, shrimp, mussels, peas, roasted red pepper, and pineapple. Yum. Or try another favorite, the Kaya burger, which is topped with pickles, avocado, bacon, tomato, Chihuahua cheese, a sunny-side up egg, and Kaya sauce. Starting any meal or happy hour with tropical guacamole—fresh avocado mixed with mango, pineapple, and cilantro—is always a yes! These flavor profiles put this guac on the sweeter side but bursting with fresh taste. Kaya offers a chance to travel to faraway lands while staying right in the heart of the city.

TIP

LOOKING TO VEG OUT?

On the third Wednesday of each month, Kaya offers a seasonal vegetarian prix fixe dinner. Vegan options are also available!

4 SMALLMAN GALLEY

SMALLMAN GALLEY is the perfect foodie destination while grubbing with others who might not have the same cravings as you. This food hall is home to four different chefs and unique restaurant concepts that create the ultimate food court experience. This is different from your typical food hall or restaurant.

Here's how you find your way around Smallman Galley. First, pick a restaurant, jump in line, order, and pay. Then grab a cocktail at the bar or a coffee at the cafe. Finally, find an open seat and wait for your food to be delivered to you. The most difficult part is picking which counter(s) to order from. Smallman's chefs come and go but not without leaving a huge impression on restaurant-goers. No restaurant is alike, making the options seem endless. This space gives local chefs the opportunity to see what it's like to run their own kitchen, hopefully one day leading to a brick-and-mortar place of their own. Iron Born Pizza, a Detroit-style pizza

TIP

GET A TASTE OF THE FULL GALLEY.

Order a starter at one counter and an entree at another. If you still have room for dessert, order from another.

joint, is a classic success story coming out of Smallman Galley. It now has two of its own spots in the city.

Each counter and kitchen inside the Galley has an original concept, so whatever you're in the mood for, you will have no problem finding something to satisfy your craving. Think gourmet burgers, or homemade pastas. Maybe tacos, or even crispy chicken sandwiches. Remember, these restaurants won't be in here forever, but if we're lucky, they just might open their own location somewhere in the 'Burgh.

5

PAMELA'S DINER

Breakfast is the most important meal of the day, and **PAMELA'S** proves it's also the most delicious. This retro diner, which has been feeding locals for over 30 years, will make you feel like you've stepped into a time machine. The nostalgic decor will surely put a smile on your face. Bright pink-and-blue walls showcase images of local and faraway icons like Roberto Clemente and Marilyn Monroe. The ultimate breakfast spot on this side of town, this is one place you can't stay away from too long; even the Obamas had to make a pit stop (more than once).

Bottomless pots of coffee, homemade hash, crepe-style hotcakes, and breakfast sandwiches to die for are a few of the things that make Pamela's world go round. The hotcakes are large and in charge, and can be ordered with sweet or savory fillings and toppings. You can never go wrong with the chocolate chip banana hotcakes, stuffed with, yes, chocolate chips, bananas, and whipped cream. Or get the hotcakes with your choice of meat, such as double-smoked thick-sliced bacon, hand-carved ham, sausage links, or turkey sausage patties.

Sunday brunch favorites like breakfast burritos, huevos rancheros, and crispy fish tacos are all perfect plates to complete a great weekend.

In addition, you can get your Sunday Funday started at the bar. The choices of vodkas to add to your Bloody Mary will certainly get you started on the right foot, with options like cucumber or red pepper vodka, or try the black pepper whiskey. Either way, you'll leave with a happy tummy.

6 BAR MARCO

BAR MARCO is a charming and refined wine bar found in a historic firehouse in the Strip, which not only offers impeccable wines and spirits but also a European-inspired menu to drool over. Menu items change seasonally to create the freshest dishes. Expect fresh pasta options with house-made sauces like sausage ragu or kale and parsley pesto. Hanger steak and salmon are also popular menu items. No matter what you decide to order here, it will always be fresh and made with only the best ingredients.

Whether you're here for brunch or dinner, Bar Marco is the perfect spot to grab a few cocktails with friends or make it a date. Aside from the craft cocktails on the menu, this bar prefers a different approach to serving its patrons' libations. Belly up to the bar or a table and order what's called a "bartenders choice" cocktail. First, decide what kind of spirit you're in the mood for—what's your go-to? Or be adventurous and try one you've never had. Then choose a flavor profile—are you into sweet or spice? Letting the bartender know what you *don't* prefer is a bonus. Once your cocktail has been ordered, be prepared to be amazed.

At Bar Marco the staff is paid by salary, so tips are not necessary. This quaint space is perfect for a celebratory evening out or a random stop by; either way both the drinks and food will not disappoint.

7 DIANOIA'S EATERY

This Italian eatery serves up some of the hottest eats in the city. **DIANOIA'S** (dee-ah-NOY-ahs) gives that home-away-from home vibe, while still dishing out some of the trendiest homemade Italian dishes this city has seen. Fresh bread, pastas, pastries, sandwiches, and pizza are made here daily. The bright and beautiful eatery is lit with blue and green glass-bottle chandeliers, with natural lighting during the day that would make any photographer giddy.

This family-owned restaurant was founded by chef Dave Anoia and his wife, Aimee DiAndrea, who know a thing or two about homemade Italian cuisine. For lunch, grab a warm panini or a whole pizza pie. The sauce is on another level. For dinner, you can't go wrong with the homemade potato gnocchi. Crank it up a notch and order it sorrentina style: served in a bread bowl with mozzarella, pecorino Romano, and basil—a carb overload worth every bite. If you save room for dessert, take a look in the dessert case

for seasonal sweet treats, as well as classics like the moist tiramisu (yes, I said moist, enjoy). If you make it for Sunday brunch, the spaghetti pie is as simple as it sounds, yet delicious and oh so photogenic (I realize I just referred to a pie as photogenic, but you'll see). Also, whether you're there for brunch, lunch, or dinner, you won't regret sipping on a cocktail or two; they don't disappoint. This little taste of modern Italy will leave you satisfied and dreaming of your next visit.

TIP

If you're looking for a quickie, head to Pizzeria Davide, directly behind DiAnoia's Eatery, for its casual eats take-out window.

THE DOWNTOWN PITTSBURGH CRAWL

1. TĀKŌ, 214 6th St., Pittsburgh, (412) 471-8256, takopgh.com

2. PORK AND BEANS, 136 6th St., Pittsburgh, (412) 338-1876, porkandbeanspittsburgh.com

3. MEAT AND POTATOES, 649 Penn Ave., Pittsburgh, (412) 325-7007, meatandpotatoespgh.com

4. PROPER BRICK OVEN & TAP ROOM, 139 7th St., Pittsburgh, (412) 281-5700, properpittsburgh.com

5. BAE BAE'S KITCHEN, 951 Liberty Ave., Pittsburgh, (412) 391-1890, baebaes.kitchen

6. THE COMMONER, 458 Strawberry Way, Pittsburgh, (412) 230-4800, thecommonerpgh.com

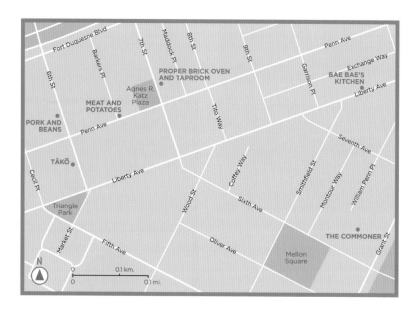

Downtown Pittsburgh

The City of Bridges

PITTSBURGH NATIVES ARE KNOWN for their fierce work ethic—it's in their blood. Monday through Friday, crowds of business professionals hustle among buildings, to and from bus stops and T stations, constantly on the move. Downtown, surrounding these busy people, are some of Pittsburgh's hottest restaurants, bars, and cafes, which are perfect for business lunches, happy hours, or just getting your grub on over the weekend. The business district stands tall with beautiful glass-and-steel skyscrapers and over 400 bridges. Though Pittsburgh is not the biggest city in the country, there is something worth seeing—or eating—on every street corner. Downtown is also home to many theaters and performance venues. On weekends and evenings, the streets are filled with people attending shows like a Broadway production at the Benedum Center or the Pittsburgh Symphony at Heinz Hall. Point State Park brings the Allegheny, Ohio, and Monongahela (aka The Mon) Rivers together in downtown and features a larger-than-life fountain at The Point. Biking, running, or strolling along the riverwalk during nice weather is a popular pastime. Because of the three rivers, kayaking and boating are two great ways to experience the full view and beauty of the city.

> In 2012, Pittsburgh transformed into Gotham City for the filming of *The Dark Knight Rises*. Batman roamed the streets in his Batmobile, and supervillain Bane blew up Heinz Field.

1

TÄKŌ

Like its name clearly states, TÄKŌ serves up some of the city's hottest tacos, but the experience goes way beyond just a yummy dish. This isn't your typical taco joint. Step inside the two-story space and you'll feel like you've entered a whole new world. The dark and chic interior has limited to no natural lighting, creating a moody ambience. Dark red light pours from the gothic chandeliers, and the octopus tentacle artwork covering the walls is an experience in itself. The self-proclaimed Asian-influenced Mexican street tacos are as unique as the vibe of this place. Serving two tacos per order, some favorites among the regulars include the octopus taco, paired with harissa aioli, baby lettuce, pico de gallo, fennel, and grapefruit. Or the Korean taco: flatiron steak, cucumber, cabbage, peanuts, and red dragon sauce for a little bite. If you're dining with a crowd, the Big Board might be your best option. Choose six pairs of tacos, presented on a rather lengthy wooden plank at the table. This way you can try a few and see which is your favorite.

Besides the tacos, you can never go wrong with a side of street corn. This plate sports sriracha mayo, cotija cheese, chili powder, and lime. Oh, and don't forget the margaritas. Nothing tops off your meal better than washing it all down with one of Täkō's unique margaritas. The spicy cucumber marg screams delicioso.

2 PORK AND BEANS

This upscale Texas-inspired barbecue joint and smokehouse serves house-smoked meats that any barbecue lover can appreciate. Before we get to the star of the show, let's talk snacks. Appetizers are hard to pass up when you're dining here, or anywhere, it's like pre-gaming your main course. Order the Korean fried ribs, rich deviled eggs, crispy pork rinds, or really anything on the appetizer list and you'll be warmed up and ready for more. For the meats, ordering a sandwich is a great option, but playing it safe. Instead, try the family-style smoked meats, served by the half pound with potato rolls and pickles, perfect for making your own sandwich. This approach makes it easy to share and try different meats. Don't forget the sides! **PORK AND BEANS** has sides that

TIP

Order family-style trays to share with the table, to get a feel for what's your favorite.

are just as delicious as the meats. Mac and cheese, burnt end baked beans, and broccoli salad give you an idea of how serious these sides are.

The aesthetic in this place will make you want to stay as long as possible. The light pink upholstered bar stools and large wooden communal tables mixed with rustic decor and dim lighting make you feel like you're in the country—smack dab in the middle of the city.

3 MEAT AND POTATOES

Ah, **MEAT AND POTATOES**, a downtown Pittsburgh staple, is also known as a weekend boozy brunch favorite. Serving both brunch and dinner, Meat and Potatoes is a trendy restaurant with some unique approaches to all-American classic dishes. For brunch, the best way to start is with an order of sticky buns for the table, along with the Bloody Mary bar, which is equipped with everything and anything one would need for the ultimate brunch beverage. Take your pick from the list of liquors, which include Old Bay vodka, jalapeño tequila, or horseradish vodka, just to name a few. These keep your cocktail interesting, but that's just the base. The fun begins at the Bloody Mary bar, where you can dress your Bloody with unlimited fresh options like cheese cubes, peppered salami, pepperoni, pickled veggies, pearl onions, shrimp, bacon, beets, or whatever your heart desires.

For dinner, options like bone marrow or pâté are encouraged. Don't worry, if these sound too intense for your liking, Meat and Potatoes has simple options like burgers, salads, and fish. If you're like me and love to share, the "Build Your Own Meat and Potatoes for Two" is a perfect option. This comes with a 45-ounce rib eye, served with bone marrow gratin and your choice of sauce, potatoes, and side. In other words, there's a feast for everyone here.

4 PROPER BRICK OVEN & TAP ROOM

If homemade Italian eats is your thing, PROPER BRICK OVEN & TAP ROOM is your place. The menu is mostly made from scratch, including the fresh mozzarella, pizza dough, and desserts. This kitchen is full of comfort food options that will appease any hungry stomach. The pizza speaks for itself. Play it safe with a Margherita pie, or channel your inner Pittsburgh pride with the Black & Gold pie: crispy Yukon Gold potato slices, cracked black pepper, red onion, roasted garlic sauce, extra-virgin olive oil, and grated pecorino Romano. Not feeling pizza? This kitchen has much more up its sleeve. The pepperoni pagnotta—a decked-out, towering pepperoni roll—will suit you just fine. Candied bacon? Yes, always! Make sure to look into the weekly specials, as the kitchen is always switching it up. Wash it all down with a cold beer or a cocktail, like a dirty martini, from the larger-than-life bar.

Sunday brunching? Perfect, Proper will still be creating pizza pies along with other drool-worthy options like the cinnamon waffle: house-made cinnamon waffle batter, berry preserves, and whipped maple butter topped with Paul Family Farms pure maple syrup. And, of course, some hair of the dog cocktails. This is a popular spot for Broadway stars to grab a quick bite or a drink before a show, considering it's right across the road from the beautiful Benedum Center for the Performing Arts. If you're lucky enough, maybe you'll run into one while you're here. This place gets packed fast, especially during dinnertime, so plan accordingly.

5

BAE BAE'S KITCHEN

To say **BAE BAE'S KITCHEN** is Instagram-worthy is an understatement. This downtown Pittsburgh Korean-inspired eatery focuses on local, healthy, and organic ingredients for all its menu options. The atmosphere is comforting, inviting, and yet so trendy. Greenery and succulents hang high and low from the walls, ceilings, and on top of the tables at Bae Bae's, perfect decor for a calm and wholesome meal. The menu isn't large, but it sure is in charge. Everything served here is beyond delicious, fresh and organic, which never goes unnoticed. Food options change seasonally, as chefs only use the freshest ingredients.

The setup is simple: Wait your turn in line and create your meal when you reach the counter. Selecting from what is in front of you might be the difficult part, as it's all so delicious. Choose either rice, noodles, or salad as a base. Then a protein—vegan and gluten-free options are available. Pick a side, and if you're up for it, some extras like kimchi dumplings or cheese wontons. In the summer, grabbing a seat outside is a must. Like inside, the greenhouse-like outdoor setup is filled with tables and greenery to make it feel as if you're in a garden tucked inside the city. Whether you dine inside or out, Bae Bae's is the perfect photo op.

6

THE COMMONER

This industrial-inspired restaurant can be found right below the Kimpton Hotel Monaco of Pittsburgh. THE COMMONER is channeling its inner upscale American tavern while keeping Pittsburgh's past close at heart. From flavors to decor, the place screams local. Black steel beams and dimmed lighting create a rustic yet sophisticated look, almost as if you've stepped back in time. Serving breakfast, lunch, and dinner every day, The Commoner is perfect for any occasion. Make sure you don't miss brunch, which happens on both Saturday and Sunday—go Commoner!

Each menu has so many options, one trip just isn't enough. Menus feature unusual twists on American classics, like the Commoner burger—a steak-blended burger with gouda, horseradish cream sauce, and crispy onions stacked between a sweet potato brioche bun. Or another classic with a twist, the pork chop. This chop rocks charred cabbage, potato latke, and Bosc pear butter. Not a meat eater? Try the tikka masala, which features sweet potato, butternut squash, tomato, chiles, yogurt, and cilantro, with wood-fired naan on the side.

The food isn't the only thing that puts The Commoner on the map. This bar is known to be fully stocked with options from 20 bar taps and beyond. These bar taps are pouring out not only your typical beer but also locally brewed beer, wine, and craft cocktails. But wait—that's not all! This bar puts other bars to shame with mixology talents and detailed garnishes galore. These cocktails change seasonally, with unique garnishes in the warmer months, The Up, Up, and Away is a must-try: Not only does it taste refreshing but it also comes with a floating balloon attached. Now *that* is picture-worthy. You won't regret ordering any beverage from this bar.

TIP

During the warmer seasons, experience the Biergarten above Hotel Monaco for European beers, German bites, and supersized games. And, of course, some fresh air.

THE SHADYSIDE CRAWL

1. GIRASOLE, 733 Copeland St., Pittsburgh, (412) 682-2130, 733copeland.com

2. ACORN, 5528 Walnut St., Pittsburgh, (412) 530-5950, acornpgh.com

3. MERCURIO'S, 5523 Walnut St., Pittsburgh, (412) 621-6220, mercuriosgelatopizza.com

4. NOODLEHEAD, 242 S. Highland Ave., Pittsburgh, noodleheadpgh .com

5. MILLIE'S HOMEMADE ICE CREAM, 232 S. Highland Ave., Pittsburgh, (412) 404-8853, millieshomemade.com/shadyside

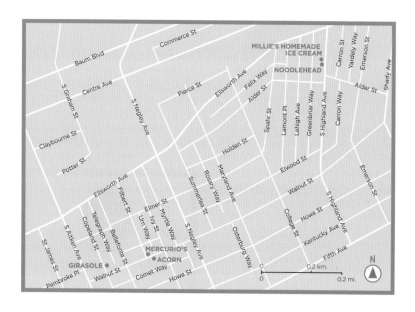

Shadyside

Our Greenwich Village

THIS PITTSBURGH NEIGHBORHOOD CAN BE FOUND JUST EAST of the city. While Shadyside is often described as quaint, it also can be described as beautiful, luxe, and even one of a kind. In summer months the streets are bordered by lush green trees, and people fill the sidewalks. Riding a bike or walking around Shadyside on a beautiful day is the perfect way to enjoy the surroundings. Many residential streets are lined with Victorian mansions, some newly renovated and some in their original glory. Fifth Avenue is where you'll find Mansions on Fifth, which is a row of breathtaking mansions including a luxury boutique hotel that is a popular venue for events and weddings. Stroll down Walnut Street to do some shopping at high-end stores like Lululemon or Williams Sonoma, or check out the unique boutiques and shops like Kards Unlimited, a storefront that sells fun gifts, books, trinkets, and, of course, hundreds of witty greeting cards. A few times a year, Walnut Street is shut down for its famous block parties: "Jam on Walnut." This event attracts over 5,000 people and offers food, drinks, and live music. Shadyside truly has the world to offer.

1

GIRASOLE

GIRASOLE, which translates to sunflower, is one of Shadyside's finest pearls. This authentic Italian restaurant can be found on a side street right off Walnut Street. Descend the steps to the brick patio packed with little tables. The French glass doors are designed with immense metal sunflower door handles and shaded with a matching rustic metal awning with Girasole etched on the front, setting the old-world tone before you even walk through the doors. Once inside this smaller space, the atmosphere will take over your senses. The dimmed lighting, charming stone walls, and copper tabletops set the mood for the ultimate romantic lunch or dinner date. If you're lucky, you might catch some charming singers serenading diners for the ultimate experience.

Expect a seasonal traditional Italian menu with some contemporary additions. An all-Italian wine list has endless options any wine lover will enjoy. Pasta dishes are, of course, a staple. Here everything is made fresh—from the perfectly prepared pasta to the meatballs that melt in your mouth, all the way to the delicious dessert. The menu depends on what's fresh, local, and available, so there may be tweaks here and there but not to fear. Everything is delicious and made with love. This place is a hot commodity, so calling ahead is preferred at peak hours, but don't be too upset if you need to wait a little. It will all be worth it in the end.

TIP

If it's a busy evening, put your name in about 20 to 30 minutes prior to your reservation, then head to a bar on Walnut for a drink to ease your wait time.

2 ACORN

This modern American restaurant thrives on serving delicious food while using the freshest ingredients possible. ACORN has a simplistic yet trendy atmosphere that will get anyone excited to experience its take on modern American cuisine. Start your weekend mornings with brunch and order a glass of fresh-squeezed OJ and a homemade bagel. This combo is a must. Also be sure to try the fresh-baked bread—carb overload and totally worth it. Build your own salad at lunch with any toppings you want, including crinkle-cut fries, which is so Pittsburgh. Top off any meal with a piece of decadent carrot cake. The icing is made to perfection but found under the cake for a deconstructed concept. Surrounding the

cake are all the classic fixings like raisins, walnuts, and, of course, carrots including the carrot tops! No waste here. The regularly changing menu features quality over quantity, and it shows through and through.

The food isn't the only thing that is being crafted from scratch. Housemade sodas and mocktails are perfect for any time of day. Enjoy the Dr. Ayer's Sarsaparilla "home remedy" soda, made with sassafras, anise, smoke, ginger, and licorice. Or, for a "merry winter walk" mocktail, the Red Riding Hood, made with cranberry, ginger, cardamom, and anise, is always a good go-to for something unique and refreshing.

3

MERCURIO'S

This family-owned and operated Italian eatery first opened its doors in 1999, starting its journey as a gelateria in Kittanning, Pennsylvania, and eventually transforming into MERCURIO'S GELATO & PIZZA in Pittsburgh in 2012.

Mercurio's serves its customers authentic Italian antipasti, salads, paninis, Neapolitan pizzas, and, of course, award-winning homemade gelato. This kitchen makes home-made gelato daily. From hundreds of different flavors, the gelateria offers 30 different flavors every day, and adds intense recipes into the rotation regularly. Some interesting flavors include mulberry cream with chocolate chunks, Fior di Latte, blueberry muffin, and stracciatella, just to name a few. The list goes on and on, which can, of course, make your job of choosing a flavor difficult! That said, you can't go wrong with any flavor. My absolute go-to is the Nutella gelato, when it's on the menu.

TIP

Take home a dough ball to create your own pie at home. Gluten-free? Mercurio's has gluten-free crust too!

Let's not forget about the food coming out of this kitchen and the pizza being baked in the stone oven. Mercurio's authentic pizzas are prepared by a Neapolitan pizza maker certified by the Italian government, meaning these pies are the real deal and cooked to perfection, with a crispy crust topped with gooey mozzarella cheese, tomatoes, extra-virgin olive oil, basil, and garlic. The aromas from these fresh ingredients will make you feel like  you're in Europe. Salads and paninis grilled on fresh house-made bread will have you salivating before you've even been served. This menu has so much authenticity, you'll be counting down the days until you go back for more.

4 NOODLEHEAD

NOODLEHEAD is, without a doubt, one of Shadyside's most prized possessions. A BYOB serving street-style Thai noodle dishes and more, it's a tranquil yet fast-paced space with an abundance of florals, greenery, and wooden accent walls that create the perfect venue to enjoy your meal. Considering how popular this eatery is, the kitchen has no other option than to hustle. Walk-ins only and no, Noodlehead does not have a phone, so don't even try. It is also cash only, but don't worry, you can find an ATM in the back of the restaurant for your convenience.

Each table is ready to rumble, with chopsticks, napkins, and, of course, sriracha ready to heat things up. Speaking of heat, when ordering your noodles you have the option of what spice level you want, from 0 to 5. Heat levels are definitely on the higher end, so order a 5 at your own risk! You also have the option of adding chicken, shrimp, or tofu. The menu has way more than just noodles, too. The snack menu is loaded with good options, but the pork belly steamed buns will change your life. These buns are like candy, and honestly, I could eat them every day for the rest of my life.

5

MILLIE'S HOMEMADE ICE CREAM

Sometimes you need a little pick-me-up, and by that I mean a scoop or four from **MILLIE'S HOMEMADE ICE CREAM**. The Shadyside location is the OG opening its doors in early 2016, but it has since opened other permanent locations and pop-up spots around the 'Burgh. Grab hold of those ice-cream-scoop door handles and let the aroma of the homemade waffle cones hit you hard the second you walk in. This social media–worthy ice cream shop is popping with pink decor and seasonal ice cream flavors that will make every visit a new experience. Of course, classics like The Best Chocolate and Chad's

Vanilla are stocked. But the unique flavors are what set Millie's above the rest, like olive oil, bananas foster, strawberry-elderflower sorbet, or fig balsamic. Millie's likes to take care of everyone, so dairy-free options are always available. Or if you're a rebel going for full dairy and need something to take the edge off, grab a lactose tablet at checkout. Now that's customer care.

Ice cream cones aren't the only things Millie's has to offer. Order a shake, or make your own sundae. The toppings seem endless with the usual rainbow sprinkles, warm chocolate sauce, and whipped cream, but there's also cocoa nibs and waffle cone pieces, which make for the perfect deconstructed cone. Jump in line quick, because Millie's is the place to be.

MILLIE'S OG LOCATION GETS CROWDED!

After getting your goodies, head to the back patio to enjoy your sweet treats.

THE EAST LIBERTY CRAWL

1. WHITFIELD, 120 S. Whitfield St., Pittsburgh, (412) 626-3090, whitfieldpgh.com

2. PIZZA TAGLIO, 126 S. Highland Ave., Pittsburgh, (412) 404-7410

3. BIRD ON THE RUN, 128 S. Highland Ave., Pittsburgh, (412) 450-8915, birdontherun.com

4. MUDDY WATERS OYSTER BAR, 130 S. Highland Ave., Pittsburgh, (412) 361-0555, muddywaterspgh.com

5. KAHUNA POKE AND JUICE BAR, 132 S. Highland Ave., Pittsburgh, (412) 450-8510, kahunapgh.com

6. DINETTE, 5996 Centre Ave., Pittsburgh, (412) 362-0202, dinettE-PGH .COM

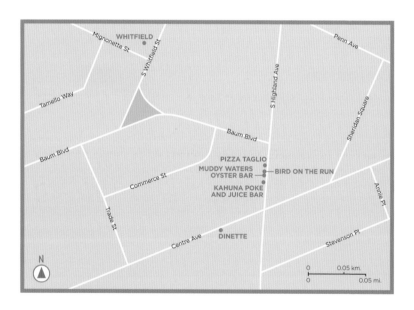

East Liberty

Where Past and Present Collide

EAST LIBERTY HAS ALWAYS BEEN AN IMPORTANT neighborhood in the city of Pittsburgh. There are so many unique fixtures to East Liberty that make it the special neighborhood it is today. With a mixture of old storefronts and new ones popping up, these streets are lined with so much to explore. Grab a salad at Honeygrow or a comfort food meal and cocktail at Kelly's Bar and Lounge. Peace, Love & Zen is a holistic wellness center that offers natural therapies including a salt cave. Grab some Pittsburgh gear at the Homage store or a coffee and pastry from across the street at Zeke's, a rustic coffee shop. Maybe your sweet tooth is asking for a milkshake from the fabulous Milkshake Factory. While visiting Pittsburgh or having a staycation, stay at one of the thriving boutique hotels like Hotel Indigo or Ace Hotel Pittsburgh. Not far from here sits Bakery Square, a shopping center with some high-end shops, delicious restaurants, and grocery stores. East Liberty is one of the busiest and best neighborhoods Pittsburgh has to offer, and it's not hard to understand why.

1

WHITFIELD

This East Liberty spot is tucked inside the Ace Hotel Pittsburgh. To start your evening, take a seat at the lobby bar and grab a drink to enjoy with some upscale bar food. Duck fat kettle corn is the perfect bar food while sipping on a beer or house cocktail. Other options while bellying up to the bar include duck leg confit, pierogies, or a cheese ball made with grass-fed cheddar. If you're lucky enough, maybe you'll catch a cute pup hanging out in this dog-friendly lobby.

Across the lobby is where you'll find the main dining room of WHITFIELD. Its modern atmosphere is minimalistic yet extremely cozy. Light wood accenting crisp white walls, lush greenery, and a fireplace make this space pretty photogenic, especially on a sunny day. The menu covers all the bases, from lots of veggie options to even more "farm-friendly" food sourced from local farms and butchered in-house. Whitfield rotates its menu with the seasons, making sure everything is in season and as fresh as possible. Duck, grass-fed beef, and trout are all popular ingredients. All steaks are served family-style and come with the option of two sides and your choice of sauce. The vegetarian side includes items like zucchini salad and roasted broccolini. Dessert seals the deal for both meat-eaters and vegetarians. Eating every meal here may seem obsessive but completely understandable.

2 PIZZA TAGLIO

If you love quality pizza, a quaint atmosphere, and a BYOB restaurant, then PIZZA TAGLIO is calling your name. The wood-fired oven is front and center of the dining room, which creates a one-of-a-kind experience. There is something special about being able to see the masters behind these pizzas create your meal right in the same room as you. Watching all the action firsthand and smelling the aromas of these pies will get your tummy rumbling. Baking these artisan pizzas doesn't take long, so get ready to eat. Once your bottle is popped, start with some fresh house-made ricotta, the perfect way to get dinner rolling. Whether you prefer red sauce–based pizza or olive oil–based pizza, Taglio has you covered. I suggest at least one of each for a table of two, or one pie per person. Sharing is caring, and mixing up flavors is always a good choice. Regardless of what specialty pie you go with, which by the way is always baked fresh and to perfection, some add-ons are a must. Mike's Hot Honey gives any dish here the perfect bite. Sweet honey with a little bit of a kick is perfect for drizzling or, in my opinion, dunking. Also, adding an egg is delicious and adds more flavor and texture. However you eat it, Taglio serves up some of Pittsburgh's favorite pizza for dinner.

TIP

If you prefer an egg with your 'za but your eating partner doesn't, ask for your cracked egg on the side. You can thank me later.

3

BIRD ON THE RUN

Do you ever crave a perfectly fried chicken sandwich? Open late seven days a week, **BIRD ON THE RUN** will always have you covered. The space is small but brings a lot to the table. Wooden tables line the walls that are covered in red-and-white chicken wallpaper, and food is served on a tray, creating the perfect rustic aesthetic. This chicken comes out hot, but you get to choose your spice level. From 0 to 4—0 being "not hot" and 4 being "hot AF"—it's up to you to choose the fate of your taste buds. A brioche bun loaded with fried chicken, mayo, and pickles may seem simple, but it's oh so delicious. If you want something a little more intense, try the Lil Chunky's chicken deluxe: topped with lettuce, American cheese, crispy bacon, pickled green tomatoes, a gooey sunny-side up egg, and spicy mayo. If chicken isn't your thing, BOTR also whips up fish sandwiches made with lettuce, tomato, and a lemon caper aioli that will knock your socks off, also served on that tasty brioche bun.

TIP

This menu has a fish sandwich that's just as delicious as the chicken!

Not only does Bird on the Run offer Turner's iced tea, a Pittsburgh classic, but it also has refreshing frozen cocktails and a lemongrass margarita made with tequila, lemongrass, agave, and lime. Any cocktail or beverage you choose will make Bird's classic chicken sandwich that much better. Whether you prefer chicken or fish, a spice level of nothing or hotter than hot, and frozen cocktails or iced tea, you'll leave this fried chicken joint stuffed and satisfied.

4 MUDDY WATERS OYSTER BAR

MUDDY WATERS, a New Orleans–inspired eatery and oyster bar, has some of the best oysters this side of the Mississippi. This raw bar is fresh and full of options from both the West Coast and the East Coast. Snacks and seafood towers are perfect for the table, like the extra-large towers holding 50 oysters, 16 shrimp, two lobster tails, and three snow crab clusters. Classic Southern sandwiches like po' boys and lobster rolls come with Cajun fries. Other classic dishes like shrimp and grits, Nashville hot chicken, gumbo, and jambalaya are all options to grub on while getting down to the jazz and blues music flowing through this small yet charming space. If you're here for brunch, weekend favorites like lobster eggs Benedict, pork belly hash, and fried chicken and biscuits will get you ready to take on the weekend.

> **TIP**
>
> Enjoy your oysters while jamming to live blues music on Tuesday and Friday nights!

Enjoying all these Southern charmed dishes calls for a craft cocktail or two to wash it all down. Along with a lengthy beer, wine, and bubbles list, this beverage menu has a craft cocktails list that features classics like the French 75, or house cocktails like Voodoo King made with Casamigos tequila, green chartreuse, pineapple, lime, sugar, egg white, and salt. If you're a fan of the bubbles, I highly suggest taking part in the Chambong, where a champagne glass is blown to work like a beer bong. Unlike your typical champagne flute, this stem curves up, and this is where you "chug" from. This makes the bubbles go down the hatch quickly, taking your brunch or dinner from relaxed to party mode. If you're lucky, snag a seat outside at the counter to enjoy a beautiful day while getting the best view of inside this perfect space.

5 KAHUNA POKE AND JUICE BAR

KAHUNA brings fresh, bright, and, most importantly, healthy food options to Pittsburgh. Health food eateries aren't as common in Pittsburgh as they are in other cities, so this poke and juice bar is perfect for anyone watching their waistline who still wants to have a good meal out and, of course, maybe a beer or cocktail. This spot is cheery, welcoming, and as their neon pink sign surrounded by multicolor shrubbery says, it's "#healthyaf." The menu features a wide variety of poke bowls with options like the kimchi salmon: loaded with green and sweet onions, pineapple, kimchi vegetables, cucumber, Korean barbecue, garlic chips, and masago. If the pre-designed bowls aren't your thing, feel free to make your own. Choose your base, protein, flavors, mix-ins, toppings, and the perfect extra crunch.

Let's not forget about the juice. Considering this is a juice bar, the beverage options seem endless. Fresh cold-pressed juices are perfect if you're on the go. Smoothies are filled with ingredients like bee pollen, honey, chia seeds, and goji berries, with the option of adding protein and other fun ingredients like matcha. Or, if you're feeling like some fun, add a shot of liquor for a small up-charge. Cocktails, wine in a can, and beer are also some beverage options for you to enjoy while washing down these filling poke bowls and getting some prime Instagram content.

6

DINETTE

This pizzeria and wine bar has been baking crisp thin-crust pizza in a crisp-looking venue since 2008. The space features an inviting atmosphere with bright-orange chairs that pop, sleek silver tabletops, a DINETTE neon sign, and paper clouds hanging high from the ceiling rafters that create quite a vision. When Dinette says it uses fresh ingredients, it's no joke. This pizzeria utilizes its roof to maintain a garden and grow tomatoes, herbs, arugula, figs, shishito peppers, eggplant, broccoli, beans, cucumbers, and melons. These ingredients absolutely shine in the pies and other dishes. The shishito peppers paired with goat cheese, fried almonds, and salt is an absolute must-try for a starter. Pies are topped with classics like ricotta and pepperoni, which are always good choices, but this menu also features pies that lift everyday ingredients to another level of perfection. The

salt-cured anchovy pizza is topped with jalapeños, which give it an extra kick of flavor, as well as capers, fresh mozzarella, and tomato. The grilled zucchini pizza features red onions, walnuts, gorgonzola, thyme from the rooftop garden, and smoked mozzarella. Dinette takes its flavor profiles to a whole new level, creating a truly remarkable experience. It's also a non-tipping restaurant; gratuities are included in the menu prices.

THE BLOOMFIELD CRAWL

1. BABY LOVES TACOS, 4508 Liberty Ave., Pittsburgh, station4744.com

2. TESSARO'S, 4601 Liberty Ave., Pittsburgh, (412) 682-6809, tessaros .com

3. BITTER ENDS GARDEN & LUNCHEONETTE, 4613 Liberty Ave., Pittsburgh, tillthebitterends.com

4. STATION, 4744 Liberty Ave., Pittsburgh, (412) 251-0540, station4744 .com

5. APTEKA, 4606 Penn Ave., Pittsburgh, aptekapgh.com

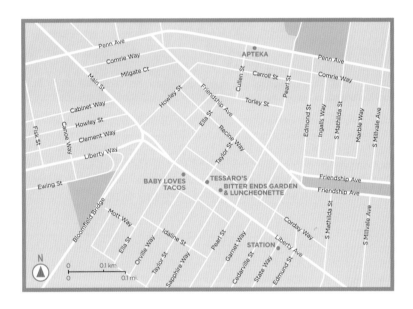

Bloomfield

Pittsburgh's Little Italy

BLOOMFIELD IS PITTSBURGH'S OWN LITTLE ITALY. Old-world culture meshed with new and innovative restaurants, bars, cafes, and storefronts is what makes this Pittsburgh neighborhood an all-time favorite. Bloomfield reflects the growth of Pittsburgh as a whole. This area has always been booming and continues to change and grow. In Bloomfield, most of the action takes place on Liberty Avenue. The area is packed with one-of-a-kind shops, markets, and cafes, like Azorean Cafe, a Portuguese cafe serving a traditional breakfast and lunch, along with imported specialties. This small neighborhood holds a big place in many locals' hearts. Every year, Bloomfield hosts one of Pittsburgh's most legendary events—Little Italy Days. This outdoor event takes place over four days with thousands of locals and visitors coming together to enjoy street vendors, traditional Italian eats, drinks, live music, and entertainment. Exploring this neighborhood and attending Little Italy Days is the perfect opportunity to get a taste of classic Pittsburgh.

1 BABY LOVES TACOS

This family-owned taco shop began its journey by hosting pop-up shops to sell their taco creations, treating Pittsburgh to some of the best tacos ever. When walking into BABY LOVES TACOS, expect a friendly atmosphere and a homey vibe. The shop is small but has big charisma. Locals share their art on the walls, and a window full of plants and greenery brings this spot to life. Aside from the friendly owners and staff, the welcoming atmosphere, and the personal touches to the space, the food is what made us locals jump for joy when the opening of a permanent shop was announced. This kitchen likes to take the fresh route, making all its salsas, slaws, and pickled vegetables in-house. Just like the shop, the menu is simple, yet exploding with personality. Six days a week (closed Sunday), diners can enjoy tacos, burritos, nachos, salads, and sides built from scratch with all fresh and locally sourced ingredients. Baby Loves Tacos also looks out for those who don't eat meat but still want a hearty meal. Vegetarian-friendly fillings like the buffalo cauliflower, barbecue mushroom, and adobo carrot options are all delicious and totally guilt-free, right? I'll take 10!

TIP

This space is tight, so plan for takeout, or grab the picnic table outside if it's available!

TIP

If you want to enjoy your tacos sitting down, check out their second space in Millvale, Pennsylvania!

2 TESSARO'S

Oh **TESSARO'S**—a Pittsburgh sports bar—home of Pittsburgh's best burger. If you disagree, you're wrong. This sports bar is exactly how you would imagine a classic Pittsburgh sports bar: exposed brick, dimly lit, Pittsburgh team details, friendly faces, and, of course, food that will make your eyes pop with amazement. Tessaro's boasts half-pound, all beef, ground chuck burgers created and shaped by an in-house butcher, then prepared over hardwood on a custom-crafted cast-iron grill. You have the option of creating your own burger or ordering one from the menu. The Gourmet Kelly Burger with bacon, grilled mushrooms and onions, and your choice of cheese is one of

TIP

Tessaro's grills up Pittsburgh's most beloved burger.

many perfect options. If you're not a burger person, don't fret. The menu is jam-packed with other options perfect for any taste buds, including a wide selection of chicken and steak sandwiches, salads, seafood, and more. No matter what you get, you'll leave Tessaro's satisfied.

3 BITTER ENDS GARDEN LUNCHEONETTE

Hurry! This menu changes fast, and I mean fast. Sometimes even more than once a day. And you don't want to miss anything the kitchen is cooking up at **BITTER ENDS GARDEN & LUNCHEONETTE**. This is a locavore-inspired kitchen, which means it uses and consumes only locally grown or produced foods and ingredients. Everything offered here reflects just that, and the menu changes based on what is fresh, local, and available. This spot is perfect for grabbing a cup of joe with a pastry, or the goat cheese and honey toast. Catch up with a couple friends over a lunch date or get some work done while you enjoy the simple idea behind Bitter Ends. Though the menu changes often, sandwiches, soups, and salads are what to expect. To create its delicious menu, Bitter Ends uses ingredients produced on a half-acre organic farm just outside Pittsburgh. Growing heirloom vegetables by

GET HERE EARLY SO YOUR OPTIONS AREN'T LIMITED.

This place is a hot commodity and can run out before closing time. Yes, it's that good.

practicing organic management skills is what makes this kitchen's world go round.

Besides the delicious food, it's the little details about this place that make it a star. After ordering your coffee, you get to pick your mug from their collection of mismatched vintage mugs. Grab some precious pastries like a glazed donut, sugar holes, or an apple-cornmeal griddle cake. Seating is limited, with a dainty counter and a few tables inside and two picnic tables covered by umbrellas outside. Everything Bitter Ends creates is handled with care and made with love. Remember, though the tasty menu items described here might not be there when you visit, a similar rendition awaits.

4 STATION

This Bloomfield restaurant features modern American cuisine for lunch and dinner, as well as a weekend brunch. Friday nights, after the kitchen closes, the bar remains open for you to continue to get your drink on. STATION is perfect for an intimate meal or just a fun night out with friends. Either way, this standout restaurant has everyone coming back for more. Inside decor features a large wooden bar, high-top tables, and black-paned-mirror walls. Adjacent to the bar is the dining room, which sports exposed brick and dimmed string lighting. The signature cocktail list is lengthy and can have any flavor profile. Cocktails range from fruity flavors to more unique tones like the D'Artagnan cocktail, made with duck fat Hennessy, gin, cherries, tropical English breakfast tea, and guava. The food can be as simple or as enticing as the cocktails, but every food and drink is served in a modern, chic way. If sharing is your ideal meal, try the small plates, like the extra-crispy wings or the honeynut squash. If you're feeling like something more substantial, the large plates such as the roasted octopus or the grilled hanger steak will fill you up. Station also serves soups, salads, and sandwiches. Brunch deals are the best deals: A set price of $29 includes a brunch cocktail and two courses of your choice.

5

APTEKA

Grab a spot in line, and if it's a busy time of night, keep an eye out for an open table or a seat at the bar to become available. If it's prime time, you might have a short wait. Once you order your food and drinks at the counter, find a seat and your order will be brought to you. Also when ordering, a tab is opened so you can order more goodies from anywhere else in the restaurant whether you're dining at an inside or outside table or sipping a drink at the bar. Oh yeah, and did I mention this menu is vegan-only? Calling all veggie lovers! If you happen to be here on a clear, warm evening, try to grab a seat in the backyard garden. The inside of APTEKA utilizes concrete and wooden details with dimmed lighting and dried flower arrangements, creating a minimalist, industrial atmosphere.

The food and drink choices from the kitchen and bar are just as unique and satisfying as the interior. What's more Pittsburgh than pierogies? These dumplings are stuffed with sauerkraut and mushrooms or smoked cabbage and potatoes. Other menu offerings might seem more intimidating, which is why asking questions is encouraged here. Along with beer and wine, craft cocktails are also available, which foster more natural flavors with ingredients like sunflower oil, poppyseeds, pear nectar, and burnt lemon, just to name a few. Even if you don't think vegan is something you would enjoy, don't knock it till you try it, because the chefs at Apteka know what they're doing.

THE OAKLAND CRAWL

1. **LEGUME BISTRO**, 208 N. Craig St., Pittsburgh, (412) 621-2700, legumebistro.com

2. **BUTTERJOINT**, 214 N. Craig St., Pittsburgh, (412) 621-2700, butterjoint.com

3. **PIE FOR BREAKFAST**, 200 N. Craig St., Pittsburgh, (412) 315-7342, pieforbreakfastpittsburgh.com

4. **SPIRITS & TALES**, 5130 Bigelow Blvd., Pittsburgh, (412) 297-4080, spiritsandtales.com

5. **THE ORIGINAL HOT DOG SHOP**, 3901 Forbes Ave., Pittsburgh, (412) 621-7388, theoriginalhotdogshop.com

6. **THE PORCH**, 221 Schenley Dr., Pittsburgh, (412) 687-6724, dineattheporch.com

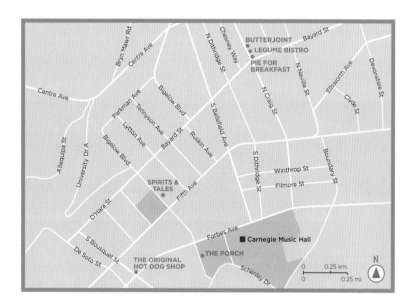

Oakland

Study Hard, Eat Harder

So many unique experiences are waiting for you in the historic neighborhood of Oakland. The neighborhood is home to three different college universities and multiple Carnegie Museums of Pittsburgh, including the Museum of Art and the Museum of Natural History. Historic landmarks include Soldiers and Sailors Memorial Hall and Museum, with a vast green lawn perfect for picnics. The Cathedral of Learning, known as "Cathy," will make you feel as if you've just walked into Hogwarts. Take a ride on the PNC Carousel in Schenley Park to bring out your inner child. This area is packed with hospitals, hotels, churches, parks, gardens, and, of course, enough restaurants and eateries to satisfy anyone's cravings. In Oakland, you'll never be bored. You'll need a couple of days just to scratch the surface of all Oakland has to offer. The streets of the neighborhood are primarily filled with students, professors, doctors, and nurses, but don't let that fool you—Oakland is one of Pittsburgh's most legendary neighborhoods. Whether you're a local or a visitor getting to know the ins and outs, Oakland will truly make you culturally richer.

1 LEGUME BISTRO

When I think of LEGUME, a few things come to mind: elegance, comfort, and grass-fed beef tartare. This New American menu also holds heavy French and Eastern European influences. Don't let the name Legume (which translates to vegetables) fool you. While the menu does, of course, feature many different vibrant and seasonal vegetables, like ramps in the spring, sweet corn in the summer, and squash in the winter, it also offers several meat and poultry options. One hundred percent of the pork, chicken, lamb, and goat coming out of this kitchen is sourced from western Pennsylvania. Other more rare meat items, which are not typically found locally, such as antelope, veal, and pheasant, are on the menu, too, along with fresh seafood.

All the details you need to know about the menu on the night of your reservation is posted online by 5 p.m. Expect options like lamb leg steak with Carolina gold rice, asparagus, and rhubarb chutney or the best (in my opinion) beef tartare in town. It's fresh and has so much flavor that once you take a bite of Legume's tartare your expectations will most likely go up a few notches. While Legume is considered to be fine dining, the atmosphere is relaxed and always welcoming.

TIP

The best beef tartare this city has ever seen!

2

BUTTERJOINT

If you are looking for Legume Bistro's unique menu but in a more casual environment, right next door is BUTTERJOINT, which is Legume's full-service bar that holds its own as one of the best spots to dine at in Oakland. Along with serving Legume's full menu, it has its own menu that features more casual but still just as delicious options. Butterjoint is known for its homemade pierogies that melt in your mouth and some of the best fresh-ground burgers in town. The Fancy Burger with gruyère, grilled balsamic red onions, and herby aioli is a game-changer. This spot is a first-come, first-served deal. The food here is simple but still bursting with flavor and creativity. The beverages are just as worthy. Butterjoint offers a lengthy list of beers, both on draft and by the bottle. A handful of these are locally brewed. The wine and bubbles menu holds its own with its diverse options. When it comes to creating craft cocktails, the sky's the limit. With both cocktails and mocktails on the menu, everyone can find a beverage to quench their thirst. This spot is known for its homemade shrub, a drinking vinegar that gives any beverage a real kick. If you're heading to Butterjoint for happy hour or dinner, prepare to leave full and completely satisfied!

3 PIE FOR BREAKFAST

PIE FOR BREAKFAST, because you only live once! And yes, this diner serves breakfast and, of course, pie all day! Just like its name, this spot has a lot of spunk. With an eclectic wall of mismatched mirror art and colors popping at every corner, you can't be anything but happy while dining here. Filled with booths, tables, and a long stainless steel counter bar lined with orange upholstered high-top stools, this is the perfect spot to start your day with family and friends, or just yourself. The moment you step through the door, you'll be hit with the aroma of house-made, salt-rising bread mixing in the kitchen. This bread is the perfect sidekick to any meal here. Load it with butter, jelly, or even eggs; it's the best vehicle for any topping and won't let you down. If you're gluten-free or vegetarian, there are plenty of options for other delicious breakfast staples. The quiche changes daily and is always fresh and fluffy. Even if you're vegan, you'll be able to find items on the menu that can be easily adjusted to fit your preference.

Let's not forget about the pie! Most of the pies in this kitchen are baked with lard and always with love. Similar to the quiches, these also change regularly, but one pie that is almost always available is the restaurant's signature pie, the vinegar pie. Don't let the name scare you. This dessert is not as intimidating as it sounds and is definitely worth a try. Most of its ingredients are the same as in your typical pies, such as eggs, sugar, butter, and the obvious one, vinegar. This pie has the texture of smooth custard and a slightly tangy taste that transitions into a sweet and oh-so-delicious bite.

TIP

SERVING PIE AT YOUR NEXT PARTY?

Call at least 48 hours in advance to place your order for an easy pickup! The Vinegar Pie is a crowd-pleaser.

With all this amazing food, you need to wash it all down with a refreshing beverage. Just like the menu, the drinks are wide-ranging, from the typical sodas, juices, beer, wines, and bubbly to mules, spritzes, and even coffee cocktails. Try the J-Town Java with Four Roses bourbon, honey, Commonplace coffee, and whipped cream, or the Hipster Doofus featuring Cynar, honey, espresso, and steamed milk. Spiked coffee is always a "yes" when you're at Pie for Breakfast.

4 SPIRITS & TALES

This brasserie-style restaurant sits above The Oaklander Hotel, with panoramic views of its surrounding neighborhood, Oakland. Serving breakfast, lunch, and dinner daily and weekend brunch, this scenic spot doesn't miss a beat. SPIRITS & TALES has a chic and sophisticated interior with black-and-white-checkered accent chairs, navy-blue suede seating, and a black marble bar with brass light fixtures and accents. This particular vibe sets this eatery above the rest, literally and figuratively. The sleek style doesn't end inside the restaurant. Head outside to the terrace to sip a cocktail and enjoy the view with a breeze. The couch and cocktail tables here are perfect for a pre- or post-meal rendezvous.

Whether you're brunching, lunching, or enjoying dinner, the S&T burger is always a good choice. A grass-fed beef patty is topped with comté cheese, oven-roasted tomato, fermented garlic aioli, and lettuce, all stacked on a challah bun. It's juicy, flavorful, and absolutely perfect. The menu is loaded with a ton of options, making it easy to dine here (though hard to choose). If you're watching your waistline, the avocado toast served with sprouts, radishes, cashew cheese, and sesame seeds is a perfect way to start your day. Some other brunch must-haves include the baked ricotta and the savory Dutch Baby. But really, in the end every choice here is the right choice.

WE SERVE YOUR
FAVORITE CONDIMENTS
ON HOT DOGS & PURE BEEF DOG
AT NO EXTRA COST...
EXCEPT CHEESE AT 98¢ A SLICE
2 SLICES   BACON $1.89
MUSTARD • RELISH • ONION • MAYONNAISE
PICKLE • CHILI • SAUERKRAUT • KETCHUP

ORIGINAL
HOTDOGS
$4.26

CHEESE DOG $5.26

Super Deluxe
Kosher Style
PURE
BEEF DOG
WITH $5.26
CHEESE 98¢ EXTRA
YOUR CHOICE OF DRESSING

Please Pay
When Ordering

**NO FOOD OR BEVERAGES
ALLOWED FROM OTHER
ESTABLISHMENTS.**

5

THE ORIGINAL HOT DOG SHOP

THE ORIGINAL HOT DOG SHOP, better known as "The O," is a family-owned business and a Pittsburgh staple. Just like its surrounding Oakland neighborhood, The O has so much history behind its years of success. Opening its doors in 1960, this old-school hot dog restaurant eventually expanded its menu to pizzas, burgers, sandwiches, subs, wings, and, of course, its famous mountains of fresh hand-cut french fries, which landed The O on CNN's "Best Fries in the USA" list. These famous Idaho potato fries have their very own ordering station, where you can make your fries a bit personal by adding fixings like gravy, ranch, ketchup, or the signature golden cheese sauce that will keep you coming back again and again. This hot dog spot also has hundreds of specialized micro, craft, and domestic beers perfect to wash all the dogs down. The Original Hot Dog Shop has been featured on the Food Network's *Unwrapped* and the PBS special *A Hot Dog Program.* Look for the iconic neon sign hung high outside the shop.

TIP

The O is one of Pittsburgh's most iconic spots to grab some grub.

6

THE PORCH

THE PORCH has a unique philosophy whereby the restaurant changes pace throughout the day, like the neighborhood that surrounds it. While the dining room is not open for breakfast, The Porch features a breakfast window that serves breakfast sandwiches, house-made pastries, espresso, cappuccino, and $1 coffee—convenience and good grub at its finest. Lunch is still casual but with a unique setup. Take a look at the menu and daily specials board, then order at the counter, grab a number and a seat, and your food will be brought to you.

For dinner and weekend brunch, The Porch doesn't hold anything back and offers full-service hospitality. Here is your chance to kick back, relax, and be fully taken care of. Service isn't the only thing this Pitt student favorite prides itself on. Local sourcing, as well as its own rooftop garden, make The Porch truly special. Order a pizza and get extra seasonings on the side for a serious DIY moment. If you're brunching, a cinnamon roll to start is a must! The daily dinner menus are large and cover a lot of bases, including grilled Atlantic swordfish, fresh salads, wraps, and gourmet burgers, just to name a few drool-worthy options. The Porch offers a full-service bar, but if you have your own bottle you're dying to pop, the staff is happy to serve your wine for a $15 corkage fee. Now that's service.

THE LAWRENCEVILLE CRAWL

1. POULET BLEU, 3517 Butler St., Pittsburgh, (412) 325-3435, pouletbleupgh.com

2. MORCILLA, 3519 Butler St., Pittsburgh, (412) 652-9924, morcillapittsburgh.com

3. DRIFTWOOD OVEN, 3615 Butler St., Pittsburgh, (412) 251-0253, driftwoodoven.com

4. ROUND CORNER CANTINA, 3720 Butler St., Pittsburgh, (412) 904-2279, roundcornercantina.com

5. SMOKE BBQ TAQUERIA, 4115 Butler St., Pittsburgh, (412) 224-2070, smokepgh.com

6. THE VANDAL, 4306 Butler St., Pittsburgh, (412) 251-0645, thevandalpgh.com

7. THE ABBEY ON BUTLER, 4635 Butler St., Pittsburgh, (412) 682-0200, theabbeyonbutler.com

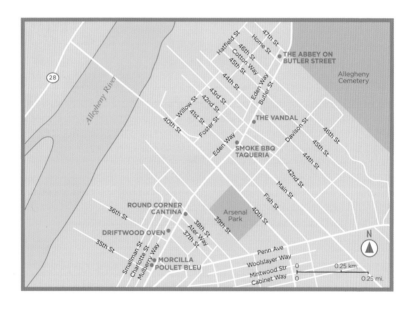

Lawrenceville

From Industrial to Chic

PITTSBURGH IS MADE UP OF MANY DIFFERENT neighborhoods, each bringing something unique to every nook and cranny of what we locals like to call the 'Burgh. Lawrenceville is no exception. It is one of the most beloved neighborhoods in town. Though the neighborhood is rather large, one street, Butler Street to be exact, takes the cake. This lengthy street is considered to be the main drag of this trendy neighborhood and is a hotbed of activity from one end to the other. Every street corner is filled with bars, bakeries, coffee shops, restaurants, boutiques, and specialty shops. You will also find the most entertaining venues to enjoy, like the world-famous Arsenal Bowl. This bowling alley has a *Big Lebowski* feel with a pinch of nightclub details like a full bar and some of the best music to get down to. Get crafty at The Candle Lab and create your own customized soy candle. Catch a movie at Row House Theater or get a new outfit and accessories at Pavement, Phoenix, or Make and Matter, to name a few shopping destinations. No matter what you're in the mood to explore, eat, or drink, you most likely won't need to stray too far off the beaten path to find what you're looking for in Lawrenceville. This trendsetting neighborhood has everything to offer and continues to grow and evolve.

1

POULET BLEU

The moment you set your eyes on **POULET BLEU**, you know you're in for an experience. This charming gated bistro greets you with gargoyles perched above a stunning courtyard, with a water fountain in the center of bistro tables creating the perfect outside dining experience. With white-and-yellow-striped awnings and blue French doors, Poulet Bleu's setting is an experience in itself. Inside, the details only become more intense. Floral wallpaper, delicate chandeliers, gorgeous mirrors mounted on the walls, fresh flower arrangements, patterned tile flooring, gold and blue accents, and an open counter concept make it feel like you've walked right out of Pittsburgh and straight into France. It's charming, beautiful, and downright delicious. From decor to dessert, I'm in love.

The menu is full of extravagant French cuisine options. If you're into escargot, do it. These snails are drenched in butter and garlic, the best way possible to eat them, of course. Poulet Bleu's French onion soup isn't your typical recipe; this one has braised oxtail, which sets it

TIP

Poulet Bleu has both patio seating and an upstairs deck, perfect for enjoying some escargot on a beautiful evening.

above any other French onion soup. Going for a cut of meat on the menu is a great deal, considering you get to choose which sauce you prefer, as well as enjoy a side of pomme frites, which like everything else are to die for. Another popular dish here is the Aligot potatoes. These cheesy potatoes were made for cheese pulls. Just you wait. Don't forget about dessert. Most importantly, if you're planning on ordering the chocolate souffle, don't forget to order it early. This bad boy takes a bit of time to bake, but it's worth it. It's pretty sizable and comes with sauces and peach ice cream. Even if you haven't saved room, you won't regret it. After your meal, head to the bar to continue sipping on some wine, beer, and cocktails.

2 MORCILLA

MORCILLA is a neighborhood favorite that is highly respected because of its unique concept and ability to make charcuterie something special. The menu features Spanish cuisine in small bites that are meant to be enjoyed family-style. This idea might turn off some, but it's a great way to get the full effect of a restaurant and experience several different dishes in one sitting. Sharing is caring, right? The menu here offers traditional **PINTXOS**, which can be described as "pick food," or small snacks you would eat in a bar. While the menu is mostly filled with these smaller options, larger, heartier plates are also available, like the Arroz Con Pitu De Caleya, which is a rice and cider-braised chicken dish, or the Bistec a la Plancha, also known as a New York strip steak prepared with mushrooms. Both of these dishes can feed up to four people. Like many other menus in Pittsburgh, the menu changes depending on what is available locally. The dimly lit, cozy space has options you won't find in other eateries. The Oxtail Montadito is simply one of the best things I have ever eaten, featuring caramelized onion and Mahon cheese. Or try the Queso en Aceite: manchego cheese with lemon, peppers, olive oil, roasted garlic, and toast. Simple enough and yet bursting with flavor. Finishing with dessert is an absolute must! The churro dessert with chocolate hazelnut fondue for dipping is the only right way to complete your meal, with an espresso, of course.

3 DRIFTWOOD OVEN

What can I say, Pittsburgh loves pizza. But really, who doesn't? If you don't, well, I feel sorry for ya. With as many pizza shops found around Pittsburgh, it might be hard to keep up. But not for **DRIFTWOOD OVEN**, which has never had a problem being on top of its game. Driftwood is a casual space with exposed brick walls, a bar, and picnic tables inside and outside when weather permits. This is not your average pizza joint. Here the art of making pizza is taken to a whole new level. Everything used to produce the menu items is local and made in-house. The doughs are naturally leavened and made with Pennsylvania-grown whole grains. The grass-fed mozzarella is pulled daily with curd from a local creamery. The fresh meats and veggies are also produced locally. Roman-style slices are available along

with 16-inch sourdough pies. Driftwood offers classic options like a pepperoni pie or a white pie, but when in Rome, Driftwood originals are highly suggested. Some favorites include the Four Cheese, which sports Grayson cheese, buttercup cheese, mozzarella cheese, pecorino cheese, Bedillion wildflower honey, and chili flakes sprinkled on top. This creamy, sweet, and spicy profile is a game-changer. Another is the Meatball Pie: Italian pork and beef meatballs, marinara sauce, herbed ricotta, garlic confit, pecorino cheese, and pickled red onion.

Pizza isn't all Driftwood knows. Other menu items are also available, including Italian meatballs, pepperoni rolls, soups, salads, and sandwiches like the Roasted Rapini': caramelized onions, fresh mozzarella, and aged balsamic on focaccia bread. Speaking of bread, Driftwood bakes and sells its sourdough hearth loaves, which are so fresh and scrumptious it will change your life. Like any other meal, finishing off your plate is best followed by something sweet. Locally made Leona's ice cream sandwiches are available.

4 ROUND CORNER CANTINA

ROUND CORNER CANTINA is literally a cantina located in a building with a round corner entryway—pretty perfect. The aesthetic inside and on the back patio is as clever as its name.

Think palm leaf wallpaper, bright-pink booths that sit as high tops, and neon and green accent colors to give it a summer feel. The front room is home to the main bar, which is where the perfectly concocted margaritas and other cocktails are created. Grab a food menu to eat here, or head to the back of the bar to take a seat in the back room in one of the rather large pink booths. But wait, there is even more space. Out in the back you'll find the cabana, which is more lounge-like with a couch and low tables. The chalet, the outside patio bar, has more high-top tables and counter space. Both spaces can be heated during the winter months, which calls for a hallelujah!

The food and drinks here are just as dreamy as the vibe. The margarita and cocktail list is full of goodies like the Lovely Rita Metermaid, made with Hornitos Blanco tequila, Aperol, grapefruit, lime, grapefruit

bitters, and salt. It has just the right amount of tart and sweet tones. Get glamorous with the Glamorous Life cocktail: Oro mezcal, Pimm's gin, lime, ginger, turmeric, and Jamaica's finest ginger . . . it almost sounds like a detox. There are different specials every day, and Saturday and Sunday brunch. Also don't miss out on the tacos. Two tacos come with each order, which may not seem like a lot, but once you get your hands on the chips and

Round Corner has different specials every single day of the week! Talk about hospitality.

salsa before your meal, you will leave feeling satisfied. Whether you order tacos, a burrito, or a quesadilla, the Nachos Supremo Grodo Gigante is the way to go if you're sharing a snack at the table. These nachos are decked out with Chihuahua cheese, cheddar cheese, refried beans, jalapeños, pico, charred corn, guacamole, and cilantro. And the chips are some of the best homemade tortilla chips around town.

5 SMOKE BBQ TAQUERIA

The thing about **SMOKE BBQ TAQUERIA** is that while it is a Mexican restaurant with some of the best flavor profiles around, it also has some of the best mac and cheese I've had to date. Random for a Mexican restaurant, right? I thought so, too, as I dug into the warm, creamy, cheesy noodles that were put in front of me. While I fangirl about the mac, let's not forget everything else on this menu. With five different queso options, ordering at least one for the table is always the right thing to do. You can never go wrong with the original queso, which is pretty basic but still fabulous. Or get a little adventurous with Some Pig Queso: pork, chorizo, bacon, poblano peppers, onions, Fresno chile peppers, and cilantro. Or the Burnt Ends Queso with wagyu brisket burnt ends, buttermilk blue cheese, poblano peppers, onions, Fresno peppers, and cilantro. These dips are on another level. If you're more into straight-up carnivorous options, meats by the pound are also available. Taco orders are served on buttermilk flour tortillas and come as singles. Your options can be as simple as an egg taco, with egg, black beans, cheese, and tomatillo sauce; or as unique as the Chicken Apple: pulled chicken, diced apples, house-made Cuban bacon, cheese, jalapeño mayo, and cilantro. If you want to wash your meal down with an adult beverage, the house cocktails and margaritas are certainly the way to go. Or if you're the designated driver, the house-made cola is the perfect substitution. It's sweet but oh so satisfying. Don't forget cash; this spot is casual and cash only. Don't worry, if you need an ATM, there's one a couple of storefronts down.

TIP

If you drink soda (or as locals here call it, pop), Smoke makes its own cola, which will please anyone's sweet tooth.

6

THE VANDAL

This simple restaurant is everything chic and tasteful. Its natural lighting and mostly all-white aesthetic make this space so dreamy. THE VANDAL is considered a cafe, and offers lunch, dinner, weekend brunch, and a prix-fixe menu for Sunday supper. The menu seems simple, but the flavors and fresh ingredients beg to differ. For lunch, options range from light fare like ricotta toast with seasonal jam to poached pear with maple cream, yogurt, and granola. If a more

hearty lunch is what you prefer, you can't go wrong with the lamb burger, which, like most of the menu options, has simple ingredients but big flavor. This guy sports cheddar cheese and tomato aioli. Most of the dishes are bright and beautiful, and detailed with edible flowers, making each dish pop with character. Also found inside is a dainty coffee bar, which gives the spare vibe a touch of warmth. The Vandal is simple, yet exquisite, and it shows the moment you step inside and again when you're looking at the menu. After seeing and tasting what The Vandal offers, you won't be able to stay away for long.

7 THE ABBEY ON BUTLER

THE ABBEY ON BUTLER is a successful gem offering a rustic, gothic coffeehouse, a large outside bistro, and a charming pub, all rolled into one refurbished funeral home. It's as unique as it sounds. By day the coffeehouse is a popular spot for freelancers to get work done while lounging on the large leather sofas in front of a roaring fireplace. The space features a magnificent antique window that was repurposed into a radiant chandelier. With exposed brick and wooden ceiling beams, you'll think you stepped into a different time. The baristas not only serve coffees and teas but also create coffee cocktails. One of my favorites on a hot summer day is the Cherry Chocolate: Disaronno amaretto and crème de cacao served iced with cold brew from Commonplace, a local coffee roaster.

Adjacent to the coffeehouse is where the pub begins. With two bars found in two different locations, this space has a larger scale. The restaurant has dark wooden flooring throughout and is filled with dimmed lighting. Paned glass windows are used to separate each room, and the lyrics to Queen's "Bohemian Rhapsody" are painted along the borders of the walls. Outside The Abbey, a gated courtyard awaits with couches for lounging, tables covered with red umbrellas, and a black swan fountain that ties in the whole area. Even though the space is large, it still feels comfortable and homey.

Whether you are dining at The Abbey for lunch, dinner, or Sunday brunch, the menu is full of comfort food. Hearty options include the fish-and-chips made with craft beer–battered Atlantic cod, served with tartar sauce and, of course, fries. Or try the homiest dish, the Mac and Cheese. These pasta shells are drenched in homemade aged cheddar cheese sauce with the option of adding chicken or fish. No matter where in The Abbey you find yourself, there is always something unique waiting.

THE MARKET SQUARE CRAWL

1. PIZZAIOLO PRIMO, 8 Market Sq., Pittsburgh, (412) 575-5858, pizzaioloprimo.com

2. BLUEBIRD KITCHEN, 221 Forbes Ave., Pittsburgh, (412) 642-4414, bluebirdkitchen.com

3. MARKET ST. GROCERY, 435 Market St., Pittsburgh, (412) 281-3818, marketstreetgrocery.com

4. FLOOR 2, Fairmont Pittsburgh, 510 Market St., Pittsburgh, (412) 773-8848, fl2pgh.com

5. SIENNA ON THE SQUARE, 22 Market Sq., Pittsburgh, (412) 281-6363, siennaonthesquare.com

6. WINGHART'S BURGER & WHISKEY BAR, 5 Market Sq., Pittsburgh, (412) 434-5600, winghartburgers.com

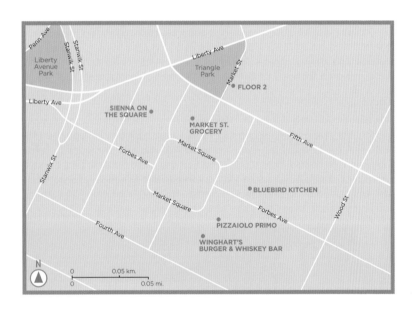

Market Square

Work Meets Play

THE COBBLESTONE STREETS THAT CREATE MARKET SQUARE are filled with the hustle and bustle of people at all hours of the workweek. Located in the heart of downtown, this part of town is always on the move and full of energy. When Pittsburgh weather decides to cooperate, bistro tables are available along with some fun outdoor activities to make any workday move along faster. Ping-Pong tables, giant chess, checkers, corn hole, and Jenga can all be found in Market Square. Live entertainment is also something common here, maybe a live band or fitness instructors leading yoga or Zumba workout classes in the center of the square. During the summer and fall months, a farmers' market takes over, selling fresh produce and goods from local vendors. Public arts projects also take place here, with artists creating detailed murals, usually using chalk. In the winter, locals take advantage of the beautiful outdoor ice rink. During the holidays, Pittsburgh Holiday Market is set up in the square. A festive market, there are vendors, restaurant pop-ups, and entertainment—even Santa visits! Market Square is lined with many unique restaurants, bars, coffee shops, bakeries, and specialty shops, like Millie's Homemade Ice Cream or Prantl's Bakery, which is known for its famous Burnt Almond Torte. Don't forget about the Original Oyster House, which hosts seasonal pop-up bars like the Zombie Bar, which is perfect considering part of the famous film *Night of the Living Dead* was filmed in Pittsburgh. No matter what season, or what time of day, Market Square is the perfect spot to grab a bite to eat and get in on the action.

TIP

The city celebrates light-up night every holiday season. Market Square is a hub for many vendors, entertainment, and family-fun activities.

1

PIZZAIOLO PRIMO

PIZZAIOLO PRIMO knows a thing or two about Neapolitan cuisine and the importance of European ambience. This two-floor authentic Italian restaurant is home to an elaborate blue-tiled wood-fired pizza oven on the first floor, which makes for a cozy and romantic experience. The second floor has a relaxed feel to it, thanks to the dark wood details and the large, rustic Tuscan-themed bar, with tall windows looking out into Market Square. The menu is filled with freshly made pizzas, pastas, salads, and so many more options for lunch and dinner, along with a wine, beer, and cocktail list that is big enough to make you feel like you're in a store, not a restaurant. If you make it to Primo for happy hour, which runs from 4:30 to 6:30 p.m. Monday through Friday, or Sunday from 4 to 6 p.m., grab a seat at the bar for some crispy, cheesy arancini or a melt-in-your-mouth Margherita pizza. There are also specials on calamari and meatballs. What's happy hour without some drinks, right? With options like an Aperol spritz, Peroni (an Italian beer on draft), and local draft beers, you'll leave this happy hour well-hydrated. Well, at least not thirsty.

TIP

Hustle to the upstairs bar quickly to snag a seat for a weekday happy hour. These seats fill up fast!

2 BLUEBIRD KITCHEN

If you work downtown, especially in the Market Square area, then there is a solid chance BLUEBIRD KITCHEN is your breakfast and lunch spot of choice. Bluebird Kitchen is a one-stop shop for a satisfying quick breakfast, lunch, or just a little pick-me-up during your day. The food here is designed to be enjoyed on the go, yet the options are always nutritious and, of course, delicious. Bluebird has created a prime spot for locals and visitors to enjoy something quick, but also something that makes customers want to take a break and enjoy the small things in life. You'll find things on the menu like homemade pastries, freshly squeezed orange juice, or sandwiches on bread that's made in-house. Everything here is made from scratch, and there are many gluten-free or vegan options. Selections change daily, as Bluebird uses only local, high-quality products. The kitchen always purchases its goods from small, local purveyors that operate at the same level of care and compassion when it comes to serving their customers. Major kudos to these guys.

Breakfast is served until 10:30 a.m. Monday through Friday. Though the menu changes regularly, expect some classics like a local fried egg sandwich, or stoneground Southern grits, which is served with bacon, cheddar cheese, and two fried eggs. For lunch, enjoy a cold or hot sandwich, soup and salad, or a more substantial side, like a pasta or veggie salad. No matter what time of day, walking into Bluebird Kitchen will probably be the highlight of your day.

3 MARKET ST. GROCERY

There are so many elements happening at **MARKET ST. GROCERY**, and every single aspect just works. This is a one-of-a-kind spot, especially in this part of town. Here you can grab a casual lunch or dinner to-go or something quick at the coffee bar. Better yet, grab a seat in the wine bar for brunch or happy hour, aka the finer times in life. But wait, there's more, lots more. Surrounding all this is a market! This makes it so convenient if you need to grab some groceries for the week or something for dinner. Market St. has fresh produce and pantry staples like oils, vinegar, crackers, and snacks, fresh cheeses, fresh bread and other baked goods, house-made cold cuts, ice cream, milk, juices, sodas, and flowers. The list goes on and on. It even has a Gaby et Jules macaron stand. The coffee bar is stocked with classic hot and cold brews, roasted with La Colombe beans from Fishtown, Pennsylvania, and serves up house-made pastries like cookies and doughnuts. Lattes are available, of course, but can be customized using homemade infused flavors. The back of the house is where you'll find the wine bar, which is stocked with all sorts of libations including local liquors and beers, along with wines imported directly from Abruzzo, Italy. Wines can be purchased by the glass, bottle, or case. Enjoying these refreshments with cheese and charcuterie plates is the best way to end your day, or start your evening.

TIP

Pick up a quick and wholesome lunch while also picking up your weekly specialty groceries, ingredients, desserts, and fresh blooms.

Market St. Grocery takes its cue from neighborhood markets of the past but still manages to maintain a unique and modern feel. If you're only stopping in to grab a meal, made-to-order specialty sandwiches are available, like the chicken pesto sandwich, topped with grilled chicken, pesto, provolone cheese, fresh tomato, pickled onions, and greens. Warm prepared dishes are made in-house daily. Some popular options include salmon, roasted chicken, pasta, and soups. Selections change daily, but no matter what is being served, Market St. Grocery is always killing it.

4 FLOOR 2

This standout space is on the second floor of the Fairmont Hotel in Market Square. The moment you set eyes on the large and bold bar, you know you're in for a treat. The vibe is like nothing else in Pittsburgh. With warm hues, vintage metallic details, modern woodwork, and a brasserie-style menu, this spot is perfect for any occasion, and is a photo lover's dream. **FLOOR 2** (Fl.2) offers breakfast, lunch, dinner, and weekend brunch. Every menu has something on it that is an absolute must. In

other words, you need to try it out at each meal of the day. Breakfast is the most important meal of the day, right? Starting with a freshly squeezed juice or a fresh-pressed juice is always a yes. My favorite is the French rose, made with grapefruit, blueberries, raspberries, and watermelon. Can you say fresh? When it comes to breakfast food, something light like a coconut chia parfait with granola and mango hits the spot and can be the perfect jump-start to your day. Brunching? Then obviously a cocktail is as important as the food, like the Rise and Grind, which uses hazelnut

espresso vodka, coffee, and Baileys, topped with walnut whipped cream. Order it with the french toast, and get your camera ready. This tall toast is served with vanilla mascarpone, candied almonds, and maple syrup to drizzle over the top. It's a sight to see. Or if you're feeling adventurous, get the Chips & Ice Cream. Ice cream for breakfast? Duh! Honey caramel chips and vanilla ice cream with a dash of sea salt. I can't make this stuff up. Dinner at Fl.2 is perfect for a birthday, anniversary, or a just because date night. Whatever you order, I highly suggest a side of shoestring french fries. They are never a letdown, just like literally everything else on this menu.

5

SIENNA ON THE SQUARE

This Market Square staple is dishing out simple, modern, and delectable Italian dishes in an upscale-casual and intimate setting complete with rustic, yet chic, decor. The loft-like space is detailed with exposed white brick walls and a beautiful wooden bar that gives this restaurant a charming feel. If it's a beautiful day in Pittsburgh, SIENNA ON THE SQUARE will open the entire front area of their space, allowing inside diners to enjoy the fresh air while those taking advantage of their sidewalk seating can feel the comfortable vibe from inside. This menu consists of both classic and originally designed food options, such

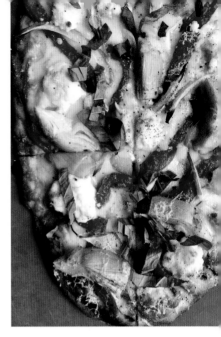

as house-made pasta and fan favorites like risotto, which at Sienna features mushrooms, zucchini, sun-dried tomatoes, shishito peppers, and whipped goat cheese, topped with fresh basil. Freshly made antipasti plates are staples here. Juicy mozzarella-stuffed meatballs are a perfect starter: made with veal, beef, pork, pine nuts, and parmesan cheese, topped with marinara. Or try the mushroom arancini: crispy warm risotto balls paired with truffle and basil pesto aioli. The menu is clearly not small and covers all the bases with flatbreads, pastas, soups, fresh fish dishes, paninis, and desserts. Menu

selections are based on the seasons and fresh and local ingredients, which shine in each dish you order. Lunch or dinner here, whether it's inside the humble dining room or outside among the city slickers, is bound to be a meal to remember. Sienna is perfect for a night out, a date night, or just an excellent happy hour to take the edge off a long day at work.

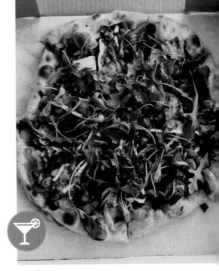

6 WINGHART'S BURGER & WHISKEY BAR

WINGHART'S BURGER & WHIS-KEY BAR began its journey as a small counter, serving its customers mouthwatering eats like pizzas, burgers, and wings fried in peanut oil. Wowza! Nothing comes out of this kitchen that's not fresh. Forget about those freezers and microwaves you see at other local bar spots. Winghart's prides itself on serving the freshest food. Everything featured on the menu is made in-house, even the sauces. Winghart's calls it a labor of love. This bar/restaurant has three locations, but the Market Square location is the OG. It doesn't feel like you're sitting at any old bar, but instead inside a cozy eatery with dimmed lighting and decorated with handmade pieces of art that serves up some of America's favorite foods. If it's a nice day, outside patio seating is available.

Grab a spot upstairs and enjoy watching the crowds of people going to and from all that Market Square has to offer while chowing down on something delicious. Start with something simple like hummus or spinach artichoke dip. Or enjoy something you don't see often enough on a menu, like the baked brie, which is paired with honey and cinnamon sugar and served with fresh fruit and flaky pita chips. Other items include pasta, wings, mac and cheese, salads, and, of course, that Pittsburgh classic, pierogies. But the burgers at Winghart's are the highlight. All are concocted with unique flavors, like the I Don't Care Whatever burger. Not only does the name of this burger speak to me, but so do the toppings: Pepper Jack cheese, cheddar cheese, crumbled blue cheese, caramelized onions, sriracha, bacon, pepperoncini, and jalapeños. My mouth is on fire just dreaming about it.

Like the food, the libations are specially cared for and tended to. Tonics, bitters, tinctures, and juices are all created fresh in-house. If you're looking for a fresh beer, or a whiskey drink, the extensive draft beer list and 70-plus whiskeys should suffice. Warning: This spot has so many delicious offerings, it's difficult to choose just a few.

THE SOUTH SIDE CRAWL

1. **CAFÉ DU JOUR**, 1107 E. Carson St., Pittsburgh, (412) 488-9695, cafedujourpgh.com

2. **DOCE TAQUERIA**, 1302 E. Carson St, Pittsburgh, (412) 238-8518, docetaqueria.com

3. **CARSON STREET DELI & CRAFT BEER BAR**, 1507 E. Carson St., Pittsburgh, (412) 381-5335, carsonstreetdeliandcraftbeer.com

4. **TOOTIE'S FAMOUS ITALIAN BEEF**, 93 S. 16th St., Pittsburgh, (412) 586-5959, tootiesfamous.com

5. **DISH OSTERIA AND BAR**, 128 S. 17th St., Pittsburgh, (412) 390-2012, dishosteria.com

6. **CARMELLA'S PLATES & PINTS**, 1908 E. Carson St., Pittsburgh, (412) 918-1215, carmellasplatesandpints.com

7. **BONFIRE FOOD AND DRINK**, 2100 E. Carson St., Pittsburgh, bonfire-pgh.com

8. **STAGIONI**, 2104 E. Carson St., Pittsburgh, (412) 586-4738, stagionipgh.com

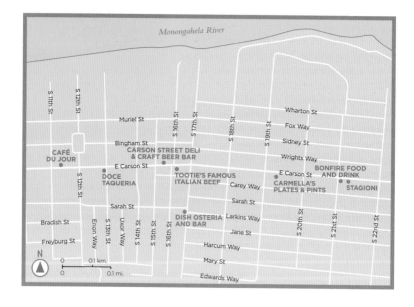

South Side

Eat by Day & Drink by Night

THIS PART OF TOWN IS BUSTING AT THE SEAMS with college students and young professionals wandering between eateries, bars, shops, and more. East Carson Street, which is considered the main drag on the South Side, is a nationally designated historic district. It's no secret that the South Side has a reputation for late-night partiers flooding the streets at wee hours of the night. The South Side is broken up into two neighborhoods: the Flats is considered the business district, and the Slopes, the residential area. Toward the end of East Carson Street is the South Side Works, which was created in the early 2000s, bringing in new apartment complexes, chain restaurants, and shops. The Works is beautiful, especially in the summer months when the fountain is on and walking shop to shop is a breeze. There is just something about East Carson Street that is so charming. The neighborhood also includes a waterfront trail that is accessible right near the Hofbrauhaus. Whether it's the old historic buildings or the locally owned and operated small businesses, Pittsburgh loves the South Side.

TIP

Hit the Southside Riverfront Park & Trail for a long stroll or bike ride, easily accessible from these streets. It's perfect after a big meal.

1

CAFÉ DU JOUR

If you're not looking for it, you might miss it. This European-inspired bistro is tucked away right in the heart of East Carson Street. Did I mention this is also a BYOB with a very affordable corkage fee? Cheers! Inside this charming eatery, head chef and owner Paul Krawiec homes in on a romantic feel with dimmed lighting and candlelit tables. If you catch this place in the warm season, be sure to head out back to eat on the brick courtyard, which has a small pond and abundant greenery. You won't believe you're in the middle of the South Side while dining out here.

CAFÉ DU JOUR offers a vibrant menu with bold flavors and colors that's been changing with the seasons since 2001. Each menu includes soups, salads, small plates, large plates, and sides, but the details of these items are switched out regularly. Soups might feature something like a wild mushroom consomme with shiitake, king oyster, porcini, maitake, and shimeji mushrooms. Other drool-worthy plates might include the slow-roasted corned beef brisket with buckwheat, braised cabbage, dried cherries, double Gloucester cheese, horseradish crema, onions, and parsley. The dishes coming from this cafe are like nothing else found on East Carson Street or perhaps in the entire city.

2 DOCE TAQUERIA

Good tunes and better tacos are perfect examples of what to expect when grubbing at DOCE TAQUERIA. Doce is known for its amazing and authentic Mexican street food and its Los Angeles flair. Head up to the counter to place your order—you can read the ornate menu, written in chalk, right above the heads of those who are creating these iconic tacos and dishes. Once you order, pay and grab a seat until they call out your name to go grab your goods. These tacos and sides are so delicious and so affordable, which means Doce is the perfect spot to satisfy your taco cravings and save money. Win-win! Doce is decked out with Day of the Dead decor year-round: neon lights that are oh-so Insta-worthy and colorful skulls and detailed murals covering almost every inch of its walls.

Each taco is made with love with your choice of flour or corn tortilla piled high with pork, beef, chicken, or vegan options topped with classic taco fixings. Daily specialty tacos are always available but tend to go fast, so don't sleep on this. If tacos aren't what you're looking for, Doce offers other delicious dishes such as loaded nachos. Pick your protein, which will be piled high over tortilla chips with nacho cheese, lettuce pico de gallo, pickled jalapeno, Cholula crema, farmer cheese, cilantro, and lime. Or try a seasonal favorite, street corn. Looking for a quick bite? Try the Walking Taco. Pick a bag of chips at checkout and fixings will be added for you, creating the perfect on-the-go pick-me-up.

3

CARSON STREET DELI & CRAFT BEER BAR

This casual dining spot stacks and wraps some of the finest and freshest sandwiches, subs, and wraps this city has ever seen, using the freshest and typically most local ingredients possible. Walk inside and the aroma of thick-cut bacon will overtake your senses—talk about pure bliss. On top of a menu that's larger than life, the CARSON STREET DELI & CRAFT BEER BAR always gets a kick out of customers creating their very own masterpieces of sandwich art, or putting their own twist on one of the menu staples. Swap some ingredients for others or just keep it as is. These sandwiches are no joke, like the Donnie Brasco: a buffalo chicken sandwich with hot pepper cheese, lettuce, tomato, onion, banana peppers, and egg salad on fresh Italian bread, topped with your choice of ranch or blue cheese dressing. Or the Three Little Pigs: sliced honey-baked ham, melted sharp cheddar, pulled pork, and bacon stacked high on a ciabatta roll. These unique masterpieces fly out of this deli's kitchen.

Carson Street Deli serves up more than just state-of-the-art sammies. Any beer snob would be proud to call this deli their go-to bar, as it offers over 300 craft beer options. With twenty locally brewed beers on draft and coolers full of bottles,

Carson Street Deli clearly likes to stick close to home. If it's a nice day, enjoy a cold crisp brew and a fresh sandwich on the back patio. Or belly up to the bar and enjoy the finer things in life, like the smell of bacon and freshly melted cheese.

4 TOOTIE'S FAMOUS ITALIAN BEEF

TOOTIE'S FAMOUS ITALIAN BEEF is the place that fulfills its customers' hungry hearts and helps satisfy their late-night cravings, especially after enjoying the nightlife along the South Side. This space is super small but dishes out sandwiches with huge flavor. The moment you step inside Tootie's, the aroma will take you back to your mother's kitchen when the Sunday roast was being prepared and your parents were yelling at you to finish your homework before dinner. This place smells just like home. Known for its juicy and delicious roast beef, Tootie's also serves chicken, sausages, peppers, mac and cheese, and more! If you hit up this spot late night, prepare to wait in line. Not only because the space is small, but also because everyone wants to get their hands on one of these sandwiches after a long night out. Don't worry, the guys behind the counter finish each order fast, so the wait is never long. All sandwiches are served with provolone cheese, and you can add sweet or hot peppers for a small up-charge. The menu is full of goodies, such as the Destroyer: loaded with beef, chicken, and sausage and covered in chili, cheese, and cornbread. Talk about intense. A major fan favorite is the Chicken Mac n' Cheese. This sandwich is loaded with pulled chicken and provolone cheese and topped with bacon mac n' cheese. It's pretty much life-changing. Grab a soda from the cooler, a bag of crispy chips, and a homemade triple chocolate brownie to complete the perfect meal.

TIP

I personally skip the bread and order the Chicken Mac n' Cheese fixings in a bowl to enjoy with a fork.

Check out Tootie's second location in Market Square, which offers even more smoked meat options.

5

DISH OSTERIA AND BAR

The menu at DISH OSTERIA AND BAR includes classic Italian pasta dishes like its Rigatoni alla Scamorza: large rigatoni pasta with smoked mozzarella, prosciutto, peas, and roasted and salted pistachio nuts in a cream sauce with Parmigiano Reggiano, topped with freshly ground black pepper and parsley. It's creamy and absolutely bursting with flavor. El carne and fresh seafood dishes are also featured on the menu. This corner spot on South 17th and Sarah Street is tight, so plan accordingly. Belly up to the quaint bar if there is a spot available or reserve a table ahead of time. Dimly lit Tiffany chandeliers hang above the copper bar and the dining room has a casual rustic feel.

This restaurant is the perfect example of not realizing how good you have something until it's gone. When it opened its doors in 2000, local restaurant-goers immediately loved the charming OSTERIA, which usually means an affordable Italian restaurant, for its inviting character and delectable dishes. In 2017, Dish owners decided to take a well-deserved hiatus and close the doors of Dish indefinitely. This left locals at a complete loss. How were we supposed to go on without Dish? Well, lucky for Pittsburgh, Dish reopened in the spring of 2019, and we couldn't be more grateful.

6

CARMELLA'S PLATES & PINTS

One of the best parts about eating at **CARMELLA'S PLATES & PINTS** is the atmosphere. The menu is full of upscale comfort food, and the vibe matches. With dimmed lighting filling the restaurant and details like wooden-beamed cathedral ceilings, an open fireplace in the center of the main dining table, stained-glass windows, and taxidermy decor, it may seem as if you're dining in a cozy ski lodge right in the middle of the South Side. Carmella's takes its menu and cocktails as seriously as its decor. This spot serves up fresh eats from a local butcher who delivers meats daily. The menu features droolworthy ingredients that create new and original dishes. Wild game is also a menu staple here—like the Wild Game Burger, which is featured every Wednesday, or the Creamy Elk Bucatini. With the menu changing seasonally, it's best to try something new every time.

If you're looking for a great cocktail, stroll up to the bar, which just like the dining space takes the atmosphere to another level—Prohibition-style. The exposed brick bar, copper details, and liquor piled high on rustic wooden shelves take you back to another era. The bar is stocked with hundreds of whiskey options, over 100 tequilas, dozens of craft beers, wines, and craft cocktails, all on tap. Drink and eat up!

7 BONFIRE FOOD AND DRINK

This two-story restaurant concept takes over the corner of 21st and Carson Street, accommodating two very different vibes in a single space. Downstairs, expect a more casual experience, with an exposed wood-fired oven as the main conversation starter. This oven isn't just for looks but also works hard to produce some of the best flatbreads in the city, like the pesto, pear, and gorgonzola with onion jam, whose sweet and salty flavors explode when they touch your taste buds. If you're looking for a more

TIP

Mac Monday specials are
a thing, and it's making
Mondays much more
bearable.

intimate experience, the second floor of the restaurant has a small lounge area and a wine and craft cocktail bar that will impress. The second level also has a separate menu that features seasonal, modern American dishes. BONFIRE FOOD AND DRINK's menu is full of all kinds of different comfort foods. Aside from perfectly puffed flatbreads, fulfilling salads, solid sandwiches, and starters for days, mac and cheese, the comfort food of all comfort foods, makes an appearance. If you're feeling basic AF, get the Basic AF. No one will judge how boring you are, I promise. But if you have a fun palate, try the Bacon Blue Mac, with roasted shallots, maple brittle, and arugula. Brunch is all weekend long, which doesn't happen everywhere in Pittsburgh, so we locals take this into major consideration. The brunch menu has inventive items like a breakfast calzone, spiced-rum banana walnut french toast, s'mores pancakes, and ginger barbecue pork belly and grits with nori, kimchi, peanuts, and scallions. Needless to say, Bonfire is killing the flavors game.

8 STAGIONI

STAGIONI is an Italian food utopia right on Carson Street. This dimly lit eatery has two floors, with a tiny bar and dining space on the first floor and more dining space upstairs. It's a quaint space that dishes out food created from seasonal and local ingredients. The menu at Stagioni has options that will stick in your mind until the next time you get there. Traditional homemade pasta, pizza, polenta, and bread are just a few staples served here. The tagliatelle is topped with a Bolognese sauce you wouldn't believe. These thick noodles have the perfect texture and consistency, and the sauce and grana padano, a cheese comparable to Parmigiano Reggiano, make you feel like you're in Italy. If you're a cheese freak like me, the Made to Order Mozzarella is a definite go-to. Paired with prosciutto, olives, roasted peppers, balsamic, olive oil, and the perfect amount of salt dusted on top, this creamy cloud of cheese will have you cheesin' hard (see what I did there?). If you're looking for something that has fewer carbs, the pan-roasted quail with butternut squash caponata and arugula could be perfect, or a whole grilled branzino seasoned with roasted lemon, olive oil, and grey salt. The table presentation makes for a unique experience—your waiter debones your fish for you.

Aside from the most delicious menu, the wine and cocktail list are built to impress. If you're a fan of gin, I suggest the Gin e Tonica. It seems simple, but the fact that Tanqueray is paired with the house-made tonic speaks volumes, and it's as refreshing as it sounds. The menu is full of classic cocktails and more-unique ones like the Forever Summer, made with cucumber vodka, lime, St. Germain, pickled tomato juice, and Angostura bitters. Stagioni is the perfect representation of a classic Italian eatery that knows how to make unforgettable food.

THE NORTH SIDE CRAWL

1. **FEDERAL GALLEY**, 200 Children's Way, Pittsburgh, (412) 517-6400, federalgalley.org

2. **BRUGGE ON NORTH**, 40 W. North Ave., Pittsburgh (412) 226-9740, pointbrugge.com

3. **EL BURRO COMEDOR**, 1108 Federal St., Pittsburgh, (412) 904-3451, elburropgh.com

4. **LEGENDS EATERY**, 500 E. North Ave., Pittsburgh, (412) 321-8000, legendseatery.us

5. **SCRATCH FOOD & BEVERAGE**, 1720 Lowrie St., Pittsburgh, (412) 251-0822, scratchfoodbev.com

6. **PEAR AND THE PICKLE**, 1800 Rialto St., Pittsburgh, (412) 322-0333, pearandpickle.com

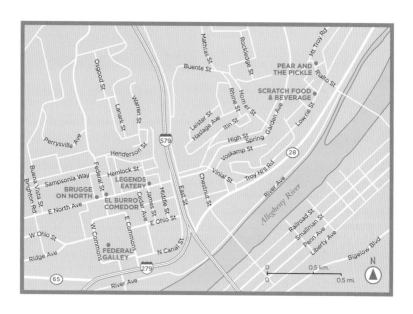

North Side

History, Sports & Cuisine

UNLIKE ANY OTHER NEIGHBORHOOD FOUND IN THE CITY of Pittsburgh, the North Side is not considered just one neighborhood. Instead, the North Side is one large area made up of many different areas, districts, and neighborhoods condensed into one iconic area. This part of town is busy and full of life. Besides restaurants and eateries, the North Side is jam-packed with attractions, businesses, and organizations that offer some incredibly unique experiences. Some of these areas include the North Shore, which is home to Stage AE, Rivers Casino, Carnegie Science Center, SportsWorks, the Andy Warhol Museum, and, of course, PNC Park and Heinz Field. Head to West Park where you'll find the iconic Gus & YiaYia'a ice ball stand, founded in 1934. The National Aviary is located in Allegheny Center just minutes away from the Children's Museum of Pittsburgh. The Mexican War Streets Historic District is where you'll find the Mattress Factory museum, a contemporary art museum, along with Randyland, a public art museum displayed entirely outside, which is considered to be one of the most colorful public art landmarks, as well as one of the most photographed places on the internet. That's right, grab your selfie sticks and get on your best side. The North Shore offers so many different experiences, perfect for working up an appetite while exploring.

1

FEDERAL GALLEY

If you guessed that **FEDERAL GALLEY** was the sister restaurant of Smallman Galley in the Strip District, then you'd be absolutely right. Unlike Smallman, Federal Galley has a couple more bells and whistles, strictly because of its location. Like its older sister restaurant, Federal fosters the same concept: a food hall featuring four different restaurant concepts and a bar flowing with adult beverages. This space and concept is perfect for a crowd. Everyone gets to choose which restaurant counter they want to order from, grab a cocktail, and then find an open seat at one of the communal-style tables. This floor can hold over 200 people. On beautiful Pittsburgh days, the garage door walls are lifted, and the rather large courtyard comes to life. Complete with many more communal tables and string lights, this is a perfect spot for happy hour, a night out with friends, brunch, and everything in between. Like Smallman, these restaurant concepts won't be in this space forever. In the past, these counters have served Detroit-style pizzas, gigantic breakfast burritos, and pancakes drenched in locally sourced maple syrup for dinner. Whenever you're wining and dining here, you know you're in for a solid meal. Each counter can rock your world.

2 BRUGGE ON NORTH

BRUGGE ON NORTH is tucked inside Alphabet City, a building that is home to City of Asylum, an establishment where readers, writers, and jazz and small-scale musicians come from around the world to find resources and inspiration. The restaurant serves lunch, dinner, and weekend brunch. Many evenings, restaurant-goers can enjoy jazz concerts and readings hosted by City of Asylum while dining or sipping on cocktails. Between the environment and the menu, Brugge on North is one of the North Side's most charming spots. The menu is known for its moules and frites (mussels and fries), which can be ordered for lunch, dinner, and brunch. Fresh from Prince Edward Island, these mussels are prepared with your choice of sauce, like a classic white wine sauce, Spanish tomato sauce, or Thai yellow curry and served with Brugge frites. Crusty bread is also served for dipping because, let's be honest, you'll want every last drop. Lunch and dinner menus offer cheese and charcuterie boards, soups, salads, sandwiches, and both small and large plates. For brunch, you can order from a menu that includes options like poutine: Brugge frites covered in bacon lardons, white wine chicken gravy, cheese curds, and pickled peppers and topped with a sunny-side up egg. Brugge also offers a special for brunch, and who doesn't love a good deal? Order the prix-fixe brunch and you can choose one entree, one side, and most importantly, a brunch beverage. No matter what time you visit Brugge, don't forget to try the moules and frites. Maybe order some bubbles and make it an event.

TIP

If you're lucky enough, you might catch live jazz music or literary readings while enjoying your moules and frites, Brugge's specialty.

3

EL BURRO COMEDOR

EL BURRO COMEDOR is a casual taqueria that gives people what they want! It's perfect for a quick bite and also serves vegan delights. I'm not talking about some simple bean-and-rice-filled taco—unless that's your thing. Of course, this menu is filled with classic taco and burrito fixings like beef, chorizo, and chicken, but as I said, this menu also features vegetarian and vegan options with more original flavor profiles. We're talking sweet potato and cauliflower tacos, vegan chorizo tacos, and potato rolled tacos, which can also be prepared vegan style. All the beans and rice coming out of this kitchen are also vegan. If you

prefer shrimp or mahimahi, El Burro has you covered, too. The space is not too big, but that doesn't mean the food can't make a big impression, which is exactly what El Burro does. These tacos and burritos have big flavor. The burritos are large and in charge, while the tacos are always filled high with flavorful fillings. Nachos, quesadillas, and other Mexican food favorites and classics are also available.

4 LEGENDS EATERY

LEGENDS EATERY is a beloved BYOB spot serving up contemporary and upscale Italian and American eats in a casual and relaxed atmosphere. This brick-and-mortar venue is found on the corner of North Avenue and James Street and has been serving hungry customers from all

over the tri-state area since 2002. The menu at Legends offers delicious finds like freshly house-made mozzarella, which is an absolute must before devouring any main course. Classic pasta dishes like penne vodka, spaghetti and meatballs, and fettuccine Alfredo share billing with other plates like chicken scallopini, chicken parmigiana, and chicken Romano. All these dishes are prepared fresh and created using locally and regionally sourced ingredients.

This North Shore favorite feels and smells like home. The open kitchen makes guests feel like they are sitting in their family's kitchen, waiting for their meal to be served. Legends runs different weekly specialty programs, like "A Night on the Town." Present your ticket or ticket stub from any Pittsburgh theater or museum that you visited that day and you'll receive a discount on your bill. Celebrate ladies night every Thursday, when ladies can enjoy an entree, dessert, and a glass of wine! Legends is the place to go to spend quality time with your favorite people over an authentic homemade meal that will be unforgettable.

TIP

OH YES, IT'S LADIES NIGHT!

Every Thursday night, ladies enjoy a specialty menu created by Chef Dan that includes an entree, dessert, and a glass of wine. Not a lady? No worries. Legends offers a different special each night!

5 SCRATCH FOOD & BEVERAGE

Troy Hill, a neighborhood in Pittsburgh's North Side, is where **SCRATCH FOOD & BEVERAGE** (F&B) calls home. Walk into Scratch and you'll catch all the feels. This cozy spot feels homey and welcoming and makes for an unforgettable experience. The menu is here is designed to delight with small plates, large plates, soups, salads, and everything in between. The food and beverage menus speak for themselves while putting new twists on New American cuisine. The restaurant offers dinner and happy hour specials along with some major entertainment. Scratch knows a thing or two about music because it hosts many shows and karaoke nights.

Scratch always offers fresh menu options, like the mushroom and rutabaga soup with flavor profiles like rosemary and pear, or beef bourguignon with whipped truffled potato, heirloom carrot, and cipollini. The menu offers gluten-free, dairy-free, vegan, and vegetarian options, creating an accessible menu for everyone, which isn't always easy to find in Pittsburgh. If you're looking for brunch, Scratch is one of Pittsburgh's better brunch options.

TIP

Grab a drink and get your vocal cords ready because Friday nights are for karaoke at Scratch.

The cocktail, beer, and wine list can quench anyone's thirst just by looking at it. The lengthy lists feature craft cocktails like the Drury Lane, made with Korbel brandy, lemon, ginger,

and aromatic bitters. Local beers and other beverages are on draft, including Red Star, a locally brewed kombucha that is a step ahead of the rest. Snaps for Scratch! These beverage lists are perfect, especially when you're trying to get a serious karaoke session in. If karaoke isn't particularly your thing, maybe some liquid courage will get you in the mood.

6 PEAR AND THE PICKLE

If you're a breakfast sandwich any time of day kind of person, PEAR AND THE PICKLE is where you want to be. Hike up Rialto Street, a hill that Pittsburgh locals might shrug their shoulders at and that most likely will cause a brief panic for visitors who aren't used to Pittsburgh hills. Making your way up this street will be well worth it. Pear and the Pickle is a dreamy cafe that serves freshly prepared foods all day long, including hot and cold sandwiches, soups, salads, and baked goods. Lots of windows, hardwood floors, wooden tables of all sizes with mismatched chairs, and freshly picked flowers make this space the perfect workplace for someone who works out of coffee shops, or for anyone looking to enjoy themselves over a cup of joe and a good meal. Maybe pass some time playing board games, or read the newspapers or books stacked on the bookshelf for your entertainment.

This place can get busy, especially during feeding hours, but more tables can be found toward the back of the restaurant. If weather permits, head upstairs to enjoy the cozy rooftop. Along with the classic egg, cheese, and meat breakfast sandwiches, other staples are available, like the meatloaf sandwich with pickles, lemon aioli, fresh greens, tomato, and cheese between warm grilled bread. If you enjoy more of the cold and crisp sandwich type, the Rialto is perfect: sweet sliced ham, pepperoni, hot capicola, provolone cheese, lettuce, tomato, and onion topped with Italian salad dressing. Besides crafting the best sandwiches in town, this cafe also has market essentials like eggs, deli meats and cheeses, baking powder, spices, and specialty condiments—even cleaning supplies like Comet cleaner and laundry detergent. This could make your day a one-stop shopping experience. Convenience is always bliss.

PITTSBURGH'S BEST BAKERIES CRAWL

1. **POTOMAC BAKERY**, 1419 Potomac Ave., Pittsburgh, (412) 531-5066, potomacbakery.weebly.com

2. **OAKMONT BAKERY**, 1 Sweet St., Oakmont, (412) 826-1606, oakmontbakery.com

3. **PRANTL'S BAKERY**, 438 Market St., Pittsburgh, (412) 471-6861, prantlsbakery.com

4. **THE BUTTERWOOD BAKE CONSORTIUM**, 5222 Butler St., Pittsburgh, (412) 781-0218, thebutterwoodbakeconsortium.com

5. **LA GOURMANDINE**, 4605 Butler St., Pittsburgh, (412) 682-2210, lagourmandinebakery.com

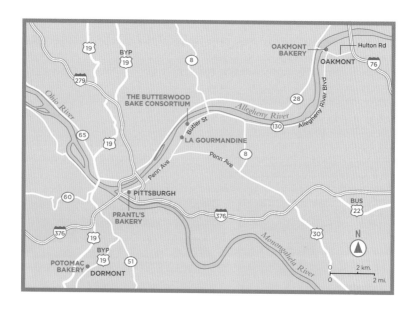

Bonus Crawl!

Pittsburgh's Best Bakeries

WHAT'S BETTER THAN STRUTTING INTO YOUR FAVORITE local bakery, knowing you're about to indulge in some of the most moist, rich, decadent, and sometimes famous cakes, pastries, and baked goods the Steel City has to offer? Basically nothing, if you ask me. Stepping foot into any bakery will undoubtedly overtake your senses: shelves and cases full of beautifully detailed cakes, old-fashioned yet classic pastry staples, the satisfying aroma of warm, freshly baked bread. There is simply nothing better than this. The Pittsburgh bakery scene has always been a special one. Family-owned storefronts have been around for decades, being passed down each generation and continuing tradition for years to come. Other local bakeries have been setting up shop in more recent years, beginning their own bakery journey and starting new traditions for locals and visitors to enjoy and to carry through in their own families. Baking is often a family affair, and the amount of love and passion that goes into all these shops' menus is as clear as day. There will always be something special about walking into a local bakery that can't help but warm your heart.

1

POTOMAC BAKERY

POTOMAC BAKERY has been dishing out some of Pittsburgh's best pastries since 1927. This family-owned and -operated classic bakery will have anyone smiling from ear to ear after tasting its famous chocolate-frosted brownies. These precious pastries are on the smaller side, so if you're like me, one is probably not enough—especially after you lock your lips on this frosting for the first time. Prepare to be blown away. Another absolute must are the decadent white icing–covered cinnamon rolls. The icing has the perfect amount of sweet with a little bit of tang. Stepping inside these doors and taking in the smell of freshly baked bread, cookies, and cakes will have you practically jumping for joy. Potomac makes it all—specialty cakes, cheesecakes, sweetbreads, coffee cakes, wedding cakes—the list goes on and on. The sky's the limit here. You can find Potomac Bakery in its original location in Dormont, right outside the Liberty Tubes (tunnels), or in Mount Lebanon in the South Hills, not far from Dormont. This bakery isn't too far off the beaten path of the city, but if it were, it would definitely be worth any hike.

OAKMONT BAKERY

OAKMONT BAKERY is not your average bakery. This award-winning, delicious destination is one of America's largest retail bakeries and one of Pittsburgh's all-time favorites. Oakmont Bakery has won national titles like "America's Best Bakeries" (Bake Magazine) and "Retail Bakery of the Year" (Modern Baking). Pick up a quick sweet treat for yourself to-go, or stick around and enjoy everything Oakmont Bakery has to offer.

When you first walk into this massive bakery, making a decision can be overwhelming. One thing is for sure, try more than one thing. When in Rome, right? Oakmont can be a hike from the city, but a long hike deserves more carbs, right? With endless amounts of beautifully piped cakes, cookies, pies, pastries, and fresh breads, you'll feel like a kid in a candy store but better, because you're in Oakmont Bakery. This larger-than-life space offers a cozy cafe finished with a fire-place, as well as inside and outside seating. The cafe offers breakfast and lunch options like cinnamon french toast, freshly baked break-fast sandwiches, hot and cold lunch sandwiches, and salads. The list of reasons to visit Oakmont is end-less, but you'll have to go see for yourself!

TIP

Skip the line and order your meal ahead online!

3 PRANTL'S BAKERY

If you haven't enjoyed **PRANTL'S** famous Burnt Almond Torte, then I only have one thing to say: Get here ASAP. This is one of the most classic tastes tucked inside the 'Burgh. This torte put Prantl's on the map decades ago, and later earned them multiple national titles like "Best Cake in America" from *Huffington Post*, "Best of Wedding Hall of Fame" from The Knot, and "Best Cake In Pennsylvania" from Food Network. This pastry star can be picked up at any of Prantl's three locations, including the Market Square and Shadyside locations. This torte is perfect for a midday pick-me-up at the office or if you're on dessert duty for a dinner party.

Prantl's offers many more classic sinful sweets, like its other famous treat, the Kaufmann's thumbprint cookie. Unlike classic thumbprint cookies with a spoonful of icing, these cookies stand tall, with a large dollop of rich icing giving these little guys their iconic look and their sweet taste. A good way to try a few of the flavors created here is by sampling the junior pastries. These miniature versions of Prantl's signature pastries, available in multiple flavors like red velvet, cookies and cream, chocolate sour cream, and white chocolate raspberry, are perfect for any sweet tooth. I hope you're wearing your stretch pants.

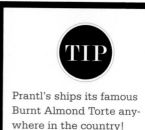

TIP

Prantl's ships its famous Burnt Almond Torte anywhere in the country!

4 THE BUTTER-WOOD BAKE CONSORTIUM

This upper Lawrenceville shop is not your typical Ma and Pa bakery. **THE BUTTERWOOD BAKE CONSORTIUM** has an atmosphere unlike anywhere else. The decor is as unique as the cakes being baked here. You'll feel like you've stepped into a Victorian mansion in a bygone era. With eclectic details like an off-white tufted French sectional sofa, deep maroon accents, large Persian rugs, Victorian mirrors, mismatched antique plates hung

high, and dried floral bouquets, the space just comes to life. With an interior like that, you won't want to leave, but if you prefer to sit outside, a small, dreamy courtyard is available in the back.

Butterwood bakes cakes and pies available by the slice, or treat yourself to an entire cake custom-made for your next celebration. These beautiful masterpieces are baked with wholesome, organic,

local ingredients including organic flour and local organic eggs. The cakes, pies, custards, and galettes are lavishly decorated with real flowers and fresh herbs. Each flavor profile is more unique than the last. Pastries and garnishes change seasonally and regularly. Similar flavors you can expect when you visit include delicious options like vegan Earl Grey cake with strawberry buttercream, Pavlova with raspberry cream and Meyer lemon curd, vegan chocolate cake with mint buttercream, or ginger cake with maple buttercream. Every cake is moist and bursting with natural flavor. Vegan options are always available. Enjoy a latte, espresso, or any of the other coffee drinks, or warm up with a hot chocolate when it's in season. Butterwood stays open late, making it the perfect place for a late-night study session or date night.

5

LA GOURMANDINE

Step inside this French bakery and in no time the aromas will lift you off your feet. **LA GOURMANDINE** is where you'll find Pittsburgh's little taste of France. Opening its doors on Butler Street back in 2010, this Pittsburgh gem now has storefronts in Mount Lebanon, downtown, and Hazelwood. This is your one-stop shop for indulging in traditional French baked goods. Baskets full of fresh-baked breads and baguettes next to a case bursting with beautiful pastries like chocolate eclairs, madeleines, gorgeous fresh fruit tarts, massive raspberry macarons as well as traditional macarons, and many other freshly baked pastries are displayed to feast your eyes first, then your taste buds. Everything may seem too pretty to eat, but you'll get past that after your first bite.

This bakery isn't just serving your sweet tooth either. Focaccia bread

is topped with mozzarella and parmesan cheese, with fresh basil and tomato sauce. French baguette sandwiches are made with fresh ingredients like butter, ham, and Swiss cheese, or butter, prosciutto, and French cornichons, for a couple of options. Quiche is always a good go-to for lunch, and is available in a vegetarian option. Using only natural and fresh ingredients, La Gourmandine serves nothing but the finest of foods, both savory and sweet. This is the perfect spot to get your fresh bakery needs for every meal of the week.

THE HONORABLE MENTIONS CRAWL

1. MEDITERRA CAFÉ, 430 Beaver St., Sewickley, (412) 740-7064,
    mediterracafe.com

2. DUNCAN STREET SANDWICH SHOP, 543 North Ave., Millvale, (412)
    252-2940, duncanst.com

3. PIGEON BAGELS, 5613 Hobart St., Pittsburgh, (412) 224-2073,
    pigeonpgh.com

4. LITTLE TOKYO, 636 Washington Rd., Pittsburgh, (412) 344-4366,
    littletokyopittsburgh.com

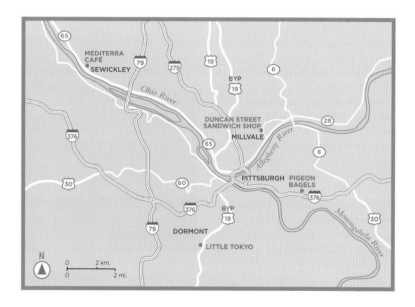

Bonus Crawl!

Honorable Mentions

Though Pittsburgh may not be considered a large city, all the goodies this city has to offer are packed tight and in close quarters. Pittsburgh and its many surrounding neighborhoods offer a great number of fun things to do, adventures to take, attractions to see, and, of course, places to eat. With so many delicious bistros, cafes, restaurants, and eateries both in and outside the city, you'll never be bored or left without anything new to try. That said, don't sleep on the neighborhoods and boroughs found just on the outskirts of the city. Whether it's a 10- or 30-minute drive, these spots are highly worth the trip. Chances are, if you're grabbing an Uber, the tab won't empty your wallet, allowing you to still splurge on feasting. These eateries and specialty shops are so special that, even though the neighborhoods in which they reside didn't make the cut, they deserve their own crawl, or shall we say, caravan? Get on your hiking shoes, fill up your gas tank, and get ready to eat well.

1

MEDITERRA CAFÉ

This dreamy cafe, bakery, and market is the definition of perfection. Black-and-white-tiled flooring, white subway tile backsplash, exposed brick, and rustic wooden accents make this spot an Instagram sensation. If it's a beautiful day, grabbing a seat at one of the red bistro tables lining Beaver Street in Sewickley is visually stimulating, as this upscale neighborhood is lined with unique shops, eateries, and locals strolling up and down the sidewalk. Fortunately, the food and beverages served at MEDITERRA CAFÉ are as amazing as its exquisite atmosphere. Stop in for the Breakfast Sammie, a brioche bun stacked with a fried egg, aged cheddar, Sicilian pesto, and arugula; add porchetta or avocado for a small up-charge. For lunch, a good go-to is the chickpea salad with cucumber, tomato, feta, herbs like dill, croutons, mesclun, and red wine vinaigrette. No matter what you get, Mediterra's pizza by the slice makes the perfect side. Wash everything down with a specialty latte or a homemade shrub—flavors change daily.

TIP

Pre-order a specialty platter for pickup to serve at your next event. It's simply not a party without charcuterie.

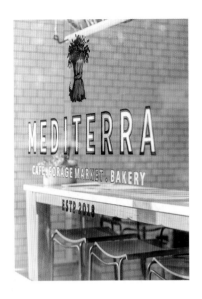

TIP

Specials change daily, and man, they are fresh.

Let's not forget about the baked goods. Mediterra creates beautiful cakes and pastries that are perfect for enjoying personally or celebrating with your favorite people. While you're picking up some breakfast or lunch, peek at the specialty market items like pasta, honeycomb, artisan bread baked in-house, and the specialty charcuterie boards. I promise you'll leave full and most likely with a bag or two of goodies to enjoy later.

2 DUNCAN STREET SANDWICH SHOP

This shop is small, but my goodness, is it serving some of the best eats this side of the city has ever seen. While **DUNCAN STREET SANDWICH SHOP** still offers its signature monthly dinners, lunch is its daily prime time. Order at the counter and, in good weather, grab a seat in the covered, dog-friendly courtyard. Just looking at the menu will give you the chills. The ingredients are all fresh, and each sandwich and side is packed tight with flavor. The "Everything" Pork sandwich features roasted pork, everything seasoning, pickled red onion jam, Boursin cheese, and

TIP

DUNCAN CATERS!

You'll be the talk of the town while hosting anything with these bites.

cucumber. Sides are all made fresh, like the chickpea salad, tossed with chickpeas, roasted sweet potato, onion, mango chutney, zhoug sauce, and almonds. These little sides go a long way.

Don't forget about your beverage. Duncan Street also brews homemade sodas. Using fresh and natural ingredients and changing things up here and there, these drinks are the perfect accompaniment for any meal. Expect unique flavors like citrus and coriander or roasted lemon. Just like everything else on the menu, desserts change regularly, but no matter what it's going to be good, like the undercooked brownies. Enough said. No matter where you are in the city, you'll want to find your way to Duncan.

3

PIGEON BAGELS

What started as a pop-up at local farmers markets, then a vendor in local cafes and coffee shops, to its very own redbrick storefront, PIGEON BAGELS is something Pittsburgh has been longing for: a specialty bagel shop. And this bagel shop is nothing short of perfection. These artisan bagels are kosher and baked fresh every day. Each spread, or schmear, however you prefer to say it, is made in-house. Build your own masterpiece by selecting your choice of bagel from options like the "everything" bagel or garlic and sea salt. Then choose your spread, which is where it gets tricky. Do you want to be a plain Jane? Or get a little wild and go for the beet? Or maybe the fig and honey? If you're

vegan, tofu schmear is also on the menu. Next up are toppings. Lox and whitefish are perfect proteins to add, along with veggies like cucumber or avocado, just to name a few.

If creating your own bagel seems overwhelming, not to worry. The menu also offers premade recipes, like the vegan carrot lox, which also comes with capers, onions, and that tofu schmear. All you have to do is decide which bagel you are worthy of. Pigeon also serves fresh brews from a local coffee company, Redhawk Coffee. The list of refreshments includes espressos, sodas, seltzers, and loose leaf teas. This is truly one of Pittsburgh's latest and greatest spots.

4 LITTLE TOKYO

Finding fresh sushi in Pittsburgh may seem like an oxymoron, but once you've tried **LITTLE TOKYO**, you will absolutely be back for more. This sushi bar and restaurant can be found in uptown Mount Lebanon, a suburb right outside the city. Pittsburgh offers easy access to public transportation like the "T," a trolley

TIP

Little Tokyo's famous ginger dressing is sold in two different sizes and is delicious on more than just salad.

that can take you all over town, including Mount Lebanon. Luckily, those taking the "T" can use the stop right across the street from Little Tokyo.

If you are a specialty roll kind of person like me, the First Date roll, rolled with shrimp tempura and topped with spicy tuna, is for you, or the rainbow roll, which gives you a taste of all the different fresh fish Little Tokyo has to offer. Other traditional hibachi dishes like chicken or shrimp are always a good option. If you're a lover of noodles, the ramen is served with Korean noodles in a hot, spicy soup broth. No matter what you order, you must try a house salad with Little Tokyo's famous ginger dressing, which is believed to lead to a long and healthy life, and so delicious you'll want to take some home. Polish off your meal with a decadent fried ice cream ball and embrace your sushi coma.

THE PIZZA JOINTS CRAWL

1. FIORI'S PIZZARIA, 103 Capital Ave., Pittsburgh, (412) 343-7788, fiorispizzaria.com

2. MINEO'S PIZZA HOUSE, 2128 Murray Ave., Pittsburgh, (412) 521-2053, mineospizza.com

3. A'PIZZA BADAMO, 656 Washington Rd., Pittsburgh, (412) 563-1000, apizzabadamo.com

4. BETO'S PIZZA, 1473 Banksville Rd., Pittsburgh, (412) 561-0121, betosoriginalpizza.com

5. SLICE ON BROADWAY, 2128 Broadway Ave., Pittsburgh, (412) 531-1068, sliceonbroadway.com

6. IRON BORN, 1806 Smallman St., Pittsburgh, ironbornpizza.com

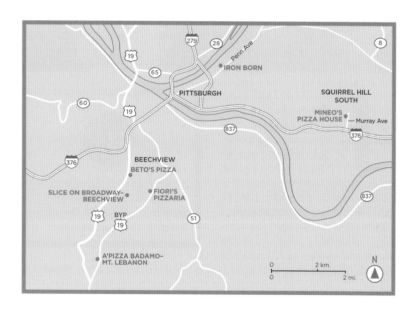

Bonus Crawl!

Pizza Joints

Pittsburgh is a city known for its three rivers, its unique Pittsburghese accent, and its pride in bleeding black and gold. Though the 'Burgh might not be best known for its pizza, locals know that the pizza this city has to offer is no joke. Those who are familiar with the pizza scene here understand that the competition can be fierce between certain shops, and the debate over who makes the best can be tense. Especially when it comes to the hottest contenders. Some pizza joints are always, and will always be, at the top because, let's be real, they simply are the best. Some Pittsburgh favorites are piled high with gooey cheese, creating more grease, which isn't necessarily a negative. Some pies are dressed with a sweet sauce, or sport baked crust and cold toppings. Others stick to the classic New York style, or offer slices big enough to feed a small family (like Benny's in the South Side). Regardless, if you're craving some 'za in the Steel City, you can't go wrong dining at any of these spots. Trust me when I say, Pittsburgh knows a thing or two about good pizza.

1

FIORI'S PIZZARIA

FIORI'S PIZZARIA is one of Pittsburgh's most beloved pizza destinations. This family-owned and -operated pizza restaurant has two locations. The first is in Brookline, right outside the Liberty Tunnels, also known as "the tubes." Fiori's is very casual with seat-yourself tables and booths, which is where you'll wait after ordering at the counter. The McMurray location is south of the city and features a more formal dining room experience. Though Fiori's offers much more than just pizza, such as calzones, wings, hoagies, spaghetti and meatballs (just to give you an idea of how large this menu actually is), the pizza is what Fiori's fans can't get enough of. Fiori's sauce is sweet, but not too sweet, the cheese is melted just right, and the crust is crispy, making these pies on point. If a plain cheese pizza isn't your thing, expect to find your toppings under the cheese. These all-natural, hand-tossed pies are made fresh every day, along with the other traditional Italian favorites. Staffers behind the counter are full of charm and hustle, a necessary skill to get these pies out as fast as possible. Just watching them work will almost make you break a sweat. This isn't your classic New York pie, but it is definitely a Pittsburgh classic.

TIP

These traditional Italian eats will have your mouth watering in no time.

2 MINEO'S PIZZA HOUSE

Opening its doors in 1958, this pizza joint is one of Pittsburgh's hottest pizza spots and doesn't plan to slow down anytime soon. Offering a full-service bar, cheesy pizza deliciousness, desserts, breakfast pizza, and so much more, MINEO'S PIZZA HOUSE of Squirrel Hill is the OG location of this pizza heaven. Two other locations can be found in the South Hills and another in the North Hills. This spot is also family-operated, which tends to be a popular trend in the pizza parlor world. The pizza is cheesy and comes out hot. The cheesy aromas will tempt you to dig right in, but be careful

TIP

This pizza is cheesy! Meaning this pizza is hot! Give it a couple blows before digging in!

not to burn your mouth. Piled high with an enormous amount of cheese, it takes a little time and a couple of big huffs and puffs to cool these slices down. Mineo's also offers a menu full of classic goodies like Italian hoagies stacked on freshly made buns from Pittsburgh's Sanchioli Bakery, stuffed banana peppers, homemade beef meatballs, and so much more, including dessert options like cannolis, cakes, and tiramisu. Mineo's is cash only so plan accordingly. If you forget, no worries, Mineo's has an ATM inside for your convenience.

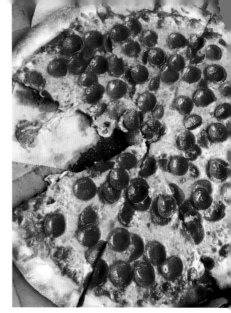

3

A'PIZZA BADAMO

A'PIZZA BADAMO calls uptown Mount Lebanon home, with another take-out location in Pittsburgh's North Side. Uptown's Badamo, with its neon "Pizza" light greeting you high above the front door, is a dine-in and BYOB spot. Inside, white subway tile and wooden benches give this spot a modern feel, yet still fosters that family-owned vibe with black-and-white family pictures and portraits covering the walls.

Inventive pizza toppings include eggplant, hot cherry peppers, meatballs, and egg. Different specialty pizzas are offered regularly, like the Wayno, topped with extra-virgin olive oil, fresh garlic, anchovies, fresh mozzarella, chunk tomatoes, black pepper, and pecorino Romano. These heavenly toppings aren't only for the pies. Caprese hoagies, tuna hoagies, pizza boats, and garlic knots are also available, just to name a few delicious items. The staff behind the counter is friendly, welcoming, and ready to hook you up with delicious pizzas and other yummy bites. The handcrafted pies Badamo has to offer will always have you coming back for more.

4 BETO'S PIZZA

This pizza is different, and being different is always a good thing. **BETO'S** sells its pizza by the slice, which is square and topped with cold cheese and toppings. Yep, you heard that right. These pizza squares are fully baked with sauce and cheese then topped with a mountain of cold cheese and any toppings you desire; the warm bottom does the rest of the work. While your plate might look like a pile of provolone, there is a pizza under it, and a dang good one. You have my word. Some might gasp, what? How? Well, it's because it's good. It's that simple. Beto's has been doing it this way for decades, and locals can't get enough. Order your desired number of pizza squares at the counter, grab a number, and wait for your pizza to be brought to you. You might want to place an order for cheese fries while you wait. It's the perfect cheesy pregame for your cheesy pizza party. This place is popular, so if you're ordering takeout, calling ahead is the way to go. Though some might be wary of cold cheese and cold toppings, Beto's is flying through 500 to 600 pounds of provolone every day, easy! Don't knock it before you try it.

TIP

These cuts are served by the slice, not by the pie. If you're hosting, a 28-cut tray should feed about 14 people!

5 SLICE ON BROADWAY

SLICE ON BROADWAY has the most locations of all the pizza spots profiled here, including at PNC Park, making it a little easier for you to get your hands on these fabulous pizzas. These pies are made from scratch and made with love. Lots of it. And that goes for pretty much everything else coming out of this kitchen. Slice on Broadway lets its display case do the talking. Step inside and feast your eyes on these handmade pies. New York–style pizza with the ability to customize your crust by choosing the traditional thin crust or a thicker crust if you prefer. Order a "ginormous"-size pie and get 16 cuts. Challenge accepted. Creating your own 'za can be tricky considering the endless variety of deliciousness. The sauces don't just consist of red and white options. Slice on Broadway makes its own green sauce using homemade basil pesto sauce, garlic, extra-virgin olive oil, pecorino Romano cheese, and pine nuts. The decisions only get tougher, as the toppings seem to have no end. Options are the key to any pizza-obsessed person. An assortment of "meaty masterpiece" pizzas and vegan pizzas are also available. The kitchen also makes breadsticks, cheese sticks, all types of rolls, salads, hoagies, and garlic knots with homemade sauces for all your dipping dreams. This is some of the freshest casual cuisine in the Steel City. Let's not sleep on dessert. If you have room, Junior's New York Cheesecake is the perfect way to polish off any meal here.

6

IRON BORN

Remember **IRON BORN**? You know, that major success story coming out of Smallman Galley in the Strip District? After its counter closed in the Galley, Iron Born opened its own brick-and-mortar shops in two locations. First, a take-out spot in Millvale, Pennsylvania, and later a full restaurant and bar in its old stomping grounds in the Strip District. This kitchen cranks out hand-forged pizzas, and locals simply can't get enough. Eight-by-ten-inch Detroit-style pizzas are cut into six pieces and decked out with house-made toppings like garlic oil and pickled banana peppers, just to give you a taste. The flavors and perfect thick, crispy crust will have anyone dreaming of these masterpieces. Is your mouth watering yet? Regular and seasonal pies can be found on the menu daily, but the white pie is anything but "regular." Topped with roasted tomatoes, onion jam, ricotta,

and lemon arugula, this bad boy will have you looking at white pizza in a whole new way. Seasonal pies come and go, but you can always expect innovative ingredients and toppings. For example, the Commonplace Coffee pie is topped with smoked pork, coffee barbecue sauce, bourbon-pickled jalapeños, and red onion. While this pie might not be around all year long, I promise something as unique will always be available here.

Square-cut pizza isn't the only thing coming out of this kitchen. Other goodies include roasted jumbo chicken wings and sandwiches like Italian, smoked pork, and short rib. What's better than munching on house-made chips with a sandwich? Maybe house-made cannoli stuffed with mascarpone and ricotta. You tell me.

COCKTAIL BARS & BREWERIES CRAWL

1. ACACIA, 2108 E. Carson St., Pittsburgh, (412) 488-1800, acaciacocktails.com

2. THE SUMMIT, 200 Shiloh St., Pittsburgh, (412) 918-1647, thesummitpgh.com

3. THE WARREN, 245 7th St., Pittsburgh, (412) 201-5888, thewarrenpgh .com

4. DANCING GNOME, 925 Main St., Pittsburgh, (412) 408-2083, dancinggnomebeer.com

5. GRIST HOUSE CRAFT BREWERY, 10 E. Sherman St., Pittsburgh, (412) 447-1442, gristhouse.com

6. HITCHHIKER BREWING CO., 1500 S. Canal St., Pittsburgh, (412) 343-1950, hitchhiker.beer

7. CINDERLANDS WAREHOUSE, 2601 Smallman St., Pittsburgh, (412) 209-1575, cinderlands.com

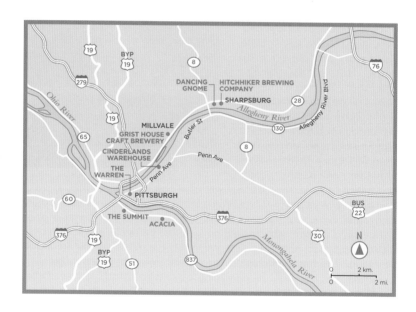

Bonus Crawl!

Cocktail Bars & Breweries

If you're visiting Pittsburgh, you're in for a real treat. The time you spend here will most likely always be a party. Whether you're here to visit friends or family, to cheer on the "Stillers" on a Steeler Sunday, or just to explore a new city, you're bound to leave longing for your next visit. What many locals know is that Pittsburgh's brewery and distillery scene is on the rise. Just like the culinary scene, these locally distilled liquors and brews deserve their name in lights. These success stories are gaining national attention due to some incredibly talented local mixologists, distillers, and brewmasters. Pittsburgh now distills multiple liquors at places such as Wigle Whiskey Distillery, Quantum Spirits, Maggie's Farm Rum Distillery, and Kingfly Spirits, just to name a few. The city is also home to breweries like local all-time favorites Brew Gentleman, East End Brewing Company, Voodoo Brewery, Strange Roots Experimental Ales, Threadbare Cider House, and Penn Brewery. The lists can go on and on. Each and every space offers something unique and is worth a visit. Whether you prefer to sip on liquor at a quaint cocktail bar or a refreshing beer at a happening brewpub, here are some go-to places to quench anyone's thirst.

1 ACACIA

Smack dab in the middle of the South Side yet just outside the insanity of it all, ACACIA is a speakeasy-inspired cocktail bar and easily one of Pittsburgh's most favorite adult beverage destinations. If you're not looking for it, you might miss it. Acacia has its windows boarded up, the front door is covered in newspaper clippings, and in good Prohibition fashion, the inside is lined with exposed brick and there's a stocked bar lit with Tiffany chandeliers pouring out hazy light. This atmosphere is perfect for sipping on craft cocktails while enjoying some good conversation. The bar may be in South Side, but don't expect to feel like you're in South Side. This isn't your typical Carson Street bar that tends to be on the wilder side. Instead, Acacia offers a calmer atmosphere while serving serious sophisticated cocktails that pair well with the cozy decor. The drinks being poured here don't just taste good but also look good, each one served in elegant glassware with the perfect garnish when appropriate. In other words, stepping inside Acacia will impress all your senses. If you're a cocktail snob, this is the place for you. The mixologists behind the bar create beverages on and off the menu using some of the highest quality and often rare ingredients. Step back to the 1920s and enjoy some of Pittsburgh's most brilliant craft cocktails, you'll be so happy you did.

2 THE SUMMIT

Jump on the Duquesne Incline, one of Pittsburgh's most famous attractions, a cable car that scales Mount Washington. Catch a ride up to the top and feast your eyes on the Grandview Lookout, which offers one of Pittsburgh's most iconic views including many bridges, rivers, the Point, and, of course, our skyline. While you're up there, check out THE SUMMIT, an intimate cocktail bar offering some of Pittsburgh's finest craft cocktails and upscale bar food. The bartenders here don't mess around when it comes to using the freshest ingredients while creating their own mixers and original cocktails. This corner bar is dreamy from head to toe. Flower boxes line the windows and overflow with beautiful blooms during warm seasons, which can be enjoyed from the inside when the garage door windows are open. High-top tables and booths line the walls, while a long bar takes center stage. The bar flows with handcrafted cocktails, and dim lighting creates a romantic feel. The kitchen works just as hard, serving up house-cut french fries that come with your choice of dipping sauce. My go-to is the roasted garlic and rosemary aioli. Even the popcorn is taken to the next level with flavors like chili lime, caramel latte, or roasted garlic and herb. If you're coming with a bigger appetite, small and large plates are perfect for sharing, or for enjoying by yourself. The Summit cooks up one of the better burgers Mount Washington has ever seen. With aged white cheddar, bacon, romaine lettuce, pickled shallots, and roasted tomato jam, this juicy baby comes with a side of those freshly cut french fries. The Summit is also stocked with cards and board games available for anyone to enjoy while polishing off some cocktails, beer, and bites. You'll never want to leave, but when you do, you'll want to take another look at the panoramic views of Pittsburgh's skyline, and all it has to offer.

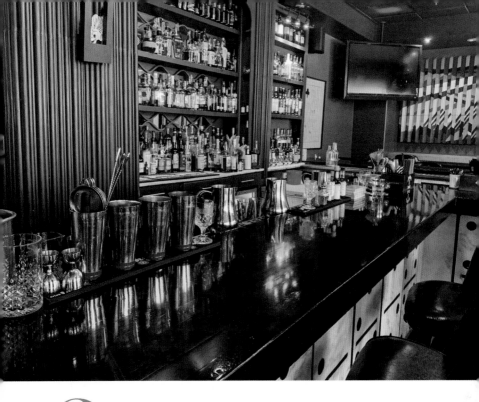

3 THE WARREN

This downtown watering hole serves up more than just craft cocktails and bar food. If typical bar bites are what you're looking for, **THE WARREN** has you covered with its drool-worthy Plain Jane Burger, chicken wings, and fresh salads. Or opt for something more cheesy and creamy, like the pimento cheese spread or crab rangoon dip, or something more unique not typically found in a bar. Sushi. Yep, this cozy cocktail bar is taking things to a new level, offering a full sushi menu with specialty rolls like the Orange Dragon Roll: shrimp tempura, cucumber, avocado, salmon, and scallions rolled up with sriracha on top. Sashimi, nigiri, and maki rolls and traditional rolls are also on deck.

Like the food menu, the cocktail menu stands out from others. Every cocktail rings in at $10 a pop. When ordering from this menu, you'll notice flavors describing the drink instead of the ingredients used to make them. Take, for example, the Fennel in Love. It's "savory, sour maple." The Warren dares you not to fall in love with this cocktail. If mixed cocktails aren't your thing, the extensive beer and wine list should suit you just fine.

The atmosphere inside these walls is just as fun and witty as the menus. With dark blue walls and jumbo domino pieces lining the bar, this warm and inviting cocktail bar might be the best reason you've lost track of time. No worries, this place is "open until 2 a.m. no matter what" every single day—their words! The Warren is the perfect spot to grab something casual to eat and something delicious to drink before or after a show downtown, or just because. Belly up to the bar and prepare for a good time. If it's your first time here, it won't be your last.

4

DANCING GNOME

DANCING GNOME is small but has made a huge impact in the Pittsburgh brewery scene. This taproom can be found in the historic neighborhood of Sharpsburg. With limited space, this place gets packed and for good reason. Dancing Gnome brews its beer right on the other side of a massive window, making it easy for patrons to see everything going on behind the scenes. The space is clean, crisp, and inviting. Grab an open seat at the bar to get a good visual of the taps available against the white subway tile backsplash. These IPAs and pale ales are some of the most prized brews on this side of the Mississippi. The beers are brewed to get the full flavor of the hops, which makes Dancing Gnome stand out from the rest. Hoppy beer may be difficult for some to enjoy, but once you get your lips on one of these beers you'll second-guess your hesitation, I know I did. The tap list rotates daily, so keep your eyes and ears open for what's available. Like the rotating taps, food trucks also change daily, which is great for changing up your experience with every visit. Even if you are not a fan of hoppy beer, don't sleep on this place, as you may discover a love for a beer you never knew was possible.

TIP

JUMP IN LINE FOR DANCING GNOME'S CAN RELEASES.

These limited-time cans go fast; sign up for the weekly newsletter to be in the know!

5 GRIST HOUSE CRAFT BREWERY

GRIST HOUSE is a craft beer brewery with some of the highest quality and most delicious beers available in town. This family-run brewery is both kid-friendly and dog-friendly. You can't get any friendlier than that! Grist House features a taproom and bars both inside and outside. This place gets busy fast, so be prepared for a wait that's well worth it. Different food trucks can be found on-site every day and change regularly, allowing you to enjoy different food with your Grist House beer. If you're a picky eater, make sure to check online ahead of time to see which food truck will be making an appearance that day. Grab a spot at a picnic table on their large, open patio and enjoy your visit under dreamy string lights, surrounded by family and friends, pups, and fresh air, all while sipping on quality beer. What more could you possibly wish for? A wide-ranging list of craft beers has options for any beer drinker. From more subtle beers to hoppier IPAs and sours, there is truly something here for everyone. If you prefer something fruity, Grist House has your back, too. Regardless of what you prefer, the time spent in this space will always be enjoyable.

TIP

Calling all dog lovers! This courtyard is very dog-friendly.

6

HITCHHIKER BREWING CO.

With two locations, **HITCHHIKER** started its journey in the heart of Mount Lebanon, a suburb just south of the city. This inside space is small, so if weather permits, grab a seat out front at the window, or head for the back patio, which is too charming to pass up. The second location is located in the historic neighborhood of Sharpsburg and offers a much larger facility in a 15-barrel brewhouse, which visitors can tour while sipping their brews. Local food trucks are available at both locations, perfect for enjoying some fresh grub with your drinks. Hitchhiker has a wide range of beer options like IPAs, double IPAs, American pale ales, stouts, sours, and other innovative flavors, such as its Box of Colors, an IPA with milk sugar and breakfast cereal. This beer is brewed with flaked oats, wheat, and milk sugar and hopped with citra and amarillo. It may sound wild, but don't knock it till you try it. All in all, Hitchhiker pours many well-rounded brews at both locations. Though some might not be available year-round, picking the brewmaster's brain about which beer is right for you is not only interesting, but you may just learn a thing or two about brewing beer.

TIP

Both locations offer food trucks, but Hitchhiker's Sharpsburg location has one every day they are open! Check out the schedule on the website for daily information.

7 CINDERLANDS WAREHOUSE

CINDERLANDS has two prime locations in the city. The first is in lower Lawrenceville, which was its first craft brewery and scratch kitchen location. This spot can be found right in the middle of the hustle-bustle of Butler Street. The second location resides in a warehouse in Pittsburgh's Strip District. Both locations offer a full restaurant experience as well as an extensive list of craft beers brewed to perfection. Forget Taco Tuesday, the warehouse location serves tacos on Monday, all day long. Other days of the week, expect a full-blown menu with lunch, snacks, dinner, and everything in between. Both locations have food menus that change periodically, but you can expect goodies like scotch eggs, pulled pork sandwiches, or classic Pittsburgh staples like haluski and pierogies.

The beer being brewed here is just as diverse as the food. From sours to hop-driven IPAs, Dad beers featuring pilsners to "Farmhouse" and "Out There" categories, even those who don't love beer have a chance to find a brew they can enjoy here. Craft cocktails, wine, locally made ciders, and even house-made sodas are also available. Cinderlands literally has it all. Yes, this is a brewery offering some of Pittsburgh's favorite beer, but it also has endless amounts of goodies perfect for the beer snob and plenty of options for those who are a little less adventurous.

Acknowledgments

Thank you! Thank you to all the amazing chefs, business owners, social media managers, and foodies from all over! I especially want to thank my family for their unconditional support: Samantha and Jimmy for picking up those late-night phone calls and answering all my editing questions, and my mom for conquering those maps. Thank you to my friends for the endless encouragement and support, and for keeping me motivated along the way. And to those who went above and beyond to help me work through this adventure. Thank you to Brittany Spinelli, Sarah Collins, and Sara Dominick for capturing so many fabulous photos. Thank you, Clara Bahan, for all your insight and willingness to help me edit all those pages. And lastly, I want to thank Mike, for all your words of wisdom and always being there for me. I am honored to have been given this opportunity, and I am beyond grateful for the new friendships built along the way.

Photo Credits

© Getty Images/iStock/titoslack: p. iii

Acorn: pp. vi (second to bottom), 32, 33

Aimee DiAndrea: pp. 14, 15

Alex Goodstein @alexeatstoomuch: pp. 97 (bottom), 112

Alisha Januck @412eatsPGH: pp. 64, 71, 79 (top), 80

Andrea Slicker: p. 148

Andrew P. Matson: p. 19

Andrew Witchey: p. 153

Anthony Musmanno: pp. 132, 133

Ariana Nathani: p. 56

Ariel Pastore-Sebring @thedependablepleasure: pp. 30, 31, 58 (top)

Bailey Allegretti: p. 154

Barbara Mates and Dan Swiderski @412lbs: p. 106

Brandon Burch @brandonbrunch: p. 68

Brittany Spinelli: pp. 24, 26, 27, 54, 55, 57, 58 (bottom), 66, 67, 82, 83, 85, 94 (top), 118, 119

Cameli Montoy: p. 140 (bottom)

Cara Delsignore: p. 109

Cheyenne Buntain @the.eating.edit: pp. vii (top), 70, 90 (top), 101, 107, 126 (left)

Christina Hrtiz @wewantfoodwednesday: p. 84 (top left)

Christopher Cook: p. 100

Courtney Bosetti: p. 79 (bottom)

Csilla Thackray: pp. 62, 63

Danielle Pellegrino @tasteohio: p. 4

Debra Cangiarella @thefork12: p. 150

Diana Kucenic: pp. 45, 46 (top left), 49 (left)

Elaine Carey @pittsburghpizza:, pp. 8, 140 (top), 142

Emilee Larimore @eatingwithmile, p. 143 (bottom)

Emily Philpot: pp. vi, 6, 7

Enrique Malfavon: pp. 2, 3 (top)

Erica Isaac: pp. 3 (middle & bottom)

Ethan Hermann: p. 104 (left)

Hannah Ogburn and Emma Curtis @girlfieris: p.10

Jacob Rubenstein: p. 18

Jason Waltenbaugh: p. 145

Jessica Iacullo @hungrygrlbigcity: pp. vii (second), 79 (middle), 84 (top right), 120

Jessica Keyser: pp. 38, 39

Karl Horn: p. 103

Katherine Whittaker @kaywhitt07: p. 11 (bottom)
Katie Ging: p. 135
Kerrington Keas: p. 5 (right)
Kitty Yohn @kitsburgheats: pp. 121 (left), 155 (top)
Laura Cobb at Elle Bee Studios: pp. 34, 35
Laura Petrilla: pp. 50, 51
Lauren M. Kucic: p. 84 (bottom)
Lisl Sukachevin: p. 36
Lorida Burkholder: p. 91
Lucy Sandstrom: pp. 88, 93
Marissa Balish @foodbabypgh: p. 59
Matt Dayak: p. 144
Megan Osborne: p. 12
Melissa A. Jones: p. 20
Michael L. Johnson: p. 37
Michael Murphy: p. 102
Mineo's Pizza House: pp. vii (bottom), 141
Miranda Piso: p. 115 (top)
Nancy Yim: p. 25 (right)
Oakmont Bakery: p. 125
Patrick Jardini: p. 105 (bottom)
Peter DeNat: p. 76
Phil Henry: p. 116
Sara Dominick @boundless_eats: pp. 9, 25 (top left and bottom), 92, 113
    (top), 136,151, 156, 157
Sarah Collins @rosecoloredcreative: p. 165
Sarah Marcucci: p. 69
Sarah Wissinger @sawissinger: p. 44
Sienna on The Square: pp. vii (second from bottom), 95
Sophia Chang @sopheating: p. 129 (top)
Stephen Kandrack: p. 115 (bottom)
Steve Derrington: p. 114
Sunny Su: p. 13
Tara Bennett @Tarabennett13 and @lifespace: p. 129 (bottom)
The Butterwood Bake Consortium: pp. 127, 128
Tom O'Connor: pp. vi (bottom), 46 (left), 47, 48, 49 (right)
Whitfield: pp. 42, 43

Index

About the Author

Born and raised in Pittsburgh, SHANNON DALY is the founder and content creator of the social media platform PittsburghPlates. Her personal and professional life revolves around everything food. Whether she is entertaining or trying a new local eatery, Shannon loves to use her passion for food and food photography. It is important for Shannon to bring together a food-focused community who share equally her passion for all things delicious. After graduating from West Virginia University, she began her foodie journey by building her brand on Instagram, which led her  to begin working closely with local PR groups and social media outlets. Currently, Shannon works with Revive Marketing Group advising on public relations support and content creation for clientele. Additionally, she contributes content for Made in PGH, an online curated platform where she writes about restaurants, small businesses, and events taking place in Pittsburgh. When she's not writing, Shannon is often networking at events or hosting parties of her own for friends, family, and her foodie community. She has an especially strong love for Halloween and hosts a party every year with the goal to one day grow it into a citywide event.